Collection Agency Secrets

EXPOSED!

Information They Don't Want You To Know

BILL COLLECTOR

Edward H. Lewis

authorHOUSE®

AuthorHouse™
1663 Liberty Drive, Suite 200
Bloomington, IN 47403
www.authorhouse.com
Phone: 1-800-839-8640

AuthorHouse™ UK Ltd.
500 Avebury Boulevard
Central Milton Keynes, MK9 2BE
www.authorhouse.co.uk
Phone: 08001974150

First published by AuthorHouse 4/21/2008

ISBN: 978-1-4259-1032-7 (sc)

Printed in the United States of America
Bloomington, Indiana

This book is printed on acid-free paper.

TABLE OF CONTENTS

Introduction..vii
The Anatomy Of A Collection Agency 1
The Anatomy Of A Bill Collector......................................3
Top 10 List Of Credit Facts For Consumers.....................4
Training Material 6
Training Material 8
Collection Agency Myths 14
Questions And Answers 16
The Fair Debt Collection Practices Act 20
The Fair Credit Reporting Act 24
A Collector's Mind-set...28
What To Do, What Not To Do 31
Your First Collection Notice 32
Disputing The Debt 35
Requesting A Payment Arrangement 36
Training Material 38
How To Avoid A Lawsuit 41
Training Material 42
What Happens If You Don't Pay...? 44
How They Find You 47
How To Get A Collection Agency To Delete Your Account: 49
How To Negotiate A Settlement And Save
    Yourself Up To 75% Of The Amount You Owe.......................51
What To Do Once You Have Settled 60
5 Steps To A Better Credit Report 62
The Test..66
This Is The True Or False Section Of The Exam.
    Please Circle The Correct Answer. 70
Do Not Send This Letter – It Doesn't Work. State Laws
    Allow Collection Agencies To Collect 3rd Party Debts –
    You Cannot Fire Them. 73
Sample Letter – Dispute / Request For Validation 74
(Sample Letter 1) – 1st Letter To Collection Agency 76
(Sample Letter 2)..78
(Sample Letter 3)..79

(Sample Letter 4)...80
(Sample Letter 5)...81
(Sample Letter 6) – Medical Collection Accounts............................83
(Sample Letter 7) – Cease And Desist 84
(Sample Letter 8) – Verification Response 86
(Inquiry Dispute) 88
File Segregation Exposed! 89
7 Ways To Eliminate Credit Card Interest 92
Secured Credit Card Marketing Scams 96
Best Overall Card 100
Fico Scores 102
Payday Loans = Costly Cash...104
Vehicle Repossession 107
Id Theftwhat's It All About?...112

INTRODUCTION

In the beginning, at the ripe-old-age of 22 I was newly married and a soon to be father of one. I never thought about the financial responsibilities of being a husband let alone a father and I had no idea the ramifications of what it would be like if I could never pay my bills, nor did I care, everything seemed to be okay. I had a perfect credit rating and had never had to deal with collection agencies before. I was working 14 hours a day, six days a week as a manager for a popular restaurant chain in Seattle Washington and I was doing fine financially, although I could barely keep my head above water, I was still making enough money each month to get by. However, I didn't have a very good health insurance plan and 3 months later when my daughter was born, well that was it. I couldn't make enough money to pay all the bills and still be able to do the things I wanted. As a matter of fact I found myself struggling from one day to the next. Now at the time I had no idea what my rights were when it came to dealing with collection agencies and believe me when I tell you, there were collections agencies calling... so it came, call after call, letter after letter, demand after demand seemed everyone wanted my money, and there was just not enough to go around. I had a family and I still had to put food on the table and diapers on the baby. Things got so bad my wife and I stopped answering the phone and we prayed for everyday to be Sunday so there was no mail or calls as most collection agencies and creditors are closed on Sunday. My credit had finally nosed dived into oblivion. The end was near and bankruptcy seemed inevitable.

Then one day I received a letter from a collection agency offering me a settlement. I was so thrilled and relieved at the prospect of maybe being able to pay one of what seemed like a hundred different medical bills, I anxiously called them. I discussed my account with the collector and all the options available to me. After making the arrangements for payment, I started asking questions to the collector as to what it was like working for a collection agency. I was amazed and a little skeptical as the collector told me about how she only works 40 hours a week and was making more money in a month than I was making in 3 months.

Seems I was in the wrong line of work. So, I decided to see if maybe I could break into the collection business. I sent resumes out to all the collection agencies in the area where I lived and was lucky to receive a job working for one of the largest agencies in the state.

A career is born. I started working in the collection industry in June of 1986 and I will never forget what that collector told me on that fateful day. She told me that if you ever want to make a lot of money and work fewer hours, become a bill collector. Now, before trashing the collection industry, it is important to understand that the debt collection industry is very much needed in this day and age. Without them, we would all be paying higher prices for everything as businesses try to recoup their losses from the consumers who didn't pay. So, I became a bill collector and she was right, I made a lot of money in this business. However, the two things she didn't tell me are the 2 reasons I'm not in that industry today. First, she neglected to tell me how depressing this business is, and the level of stress you go through is enormous. You see, as a bill collector you work on commissions, that means you earn a percentage of whatever amount of money you collect from one month to the next. So, if you have a bad month, you don't get paid, that's pretty stressful. Plus, the day-to-day fact that you're dealing with people whom for the most part cannot genuinely pay their bills is very depressing. I mean most consumers don't wake up in the morning and say "hey-let's see if I can make a bill I can't afford to pay". Therefore, once again, I have decided to change careers. I now own my own consulting firm helping people like you, understand your rights when collection agencies come knocking. However, I do have over 18 years of experience within every aspect of the collection industry, from the guy making the collection phone calls to the guy running the entire operation to the computer equipment they use. I know everything there is to know about this industry, and it's time I shared my secrets with you!

THE ANATOMY OF A COLLECTION AGENCY

What does a professional collection agency do? Collection agencies are in business for one reason only – to make money. Their only real function is to collect as much money that they can for their clients. There are various different ways they can do this, from sending dunning notices to filing lawsuits; it all depends on the individual situation.

What is a professional collection service?
A collection agency is a third-party collection service that collects past-due accounts referred to them by various credit-grantors such as credit card issuers, banks, car dealers, retail stores, healthcare facilities and any business that extends credit or offers payment installment plans. A collection agency functions with usually 5 main departments or divisions:

1. <u>SALES</u> – This is the department that makes contact with the creditors and convinces them to assign their accounts to the collection agency for a fee or percentage of whatever is collected. This department is crucial to the success of a collection agency.

2. **COLLECTIONS** – This is the department that works the accounts the sales staff brings in. They are highly trained professionals that are the backbone of the business. They are the ones who send the dunning notices and make the phone calls. They're also the ones you will be dealing with anytime you make contact with the collection agency regarding your debt. This department is crucial to the success of a collection agency.

3. **LEGAL DEPARTMENT** - This is the department that receives or will pull your file if legal action is necessary to collect the debt. They have nothing to do with the over-all collection of the debt and are advised by the collection department or the collector in charge of your account as how to proceed.

4. **<u>SUPPORT STAFF</u>** - This department is set-up to support the collection department by answering phones, filing documents and applying your payments to your account.

5. **<u>SYSTEM OPERATIONS</u>** – this is the department that enters all of the data into the collection agency computer system and they maintain the computer system to ensure there is no down time.

THE ANATOMY OF A
BILL COLLECTOR

Collectors are highly trained professional individuals that usually have an outgoing and creative personality. Because these individuals are the backbone of the business and because the over-all revenue of the collection agency depends solely on them, they are highly trained in various areas of the human psyche. For example, one of the first things they learn is to not take anything personally. They're taught not to relate to your personal problem and how to get around whatever your objection is to pay your account. They're trained how to use basic conversations to retrieve personal information from you without you realizing it. They are taught what methods to use that collect money verses what methods do not collect money. They know how to identify what type of debtor you are and what to say or do to get you to pay your bill. A good collector is trained to treat you with respect and to give you the perception that they are willing to work with you to resolve your unpaid account. They're trained when to accept a payment arrangement verses a demand for payment in full. They're taught how to analyze your financial situation and determine when to request a lawsuit and when not to request a lawsuit. They're trained on how to give you a sense of urgency to pay your bill now. They are even taught what type of voice-mail messages to leave on your answering machine that will generate the most return calls. The training a collector receives is rigorous and ongoing. I have trained collectors that today are making over 6 figure incomes. The better trained a collector is, the more money they will make and the more money they will make for the collection agency. The next few pages are inserts of an actual training guide that I created for one of the agencies I used to work for. They should give you an idea of some of the training a collector receives.

TOP 10 LIST OF CREDIT
FACTS FOR CONSUMERS

1). Unless you live in a state with community property laws dictating division/claim of assets and liabilities, prospective creditors cannot inquire about your marital status. Furthermore, prospective creditors cannot inquire about your spouse's income, unless you are claiming (both) incomes to qualify for a loan.

2). Americans spend over 70% of their gross income every year repaying debt: home loans, auto loans and credit cards.

3). Age discrimination? The actuarial tables know for sure: In the "credit scoring" game, those individuals under the age of 25 score the lowest; prospective debtors in their forties score highest, and are most desirable to lend to in the eyes of the credit grantors.

4). Owning a home debt-free doesn't necessarily score any higher than owning one with a mortgage. However, the fact that you own your home scores positive points with a prospective creditor.

5). Be aware that if you are self-employed and applying for credit, this can subtract points in the credit scoring game because of inability to verify income, tenure, etc.

6). Credit card companies divide card users into three (3) categories:

   a) Revolvers---those individuals that make the minimum payment each month;

   b) Average-----are those consumers that pay the balance off one month and the minimum balance the next.

   c) Convenience users----those consumers that pay the entire balance every month, thus avoiding interest charges (these are the least profitable to banks).

7) Over 70% of the consumers who use credit cards have no idea what interest rate they are paying on their cards.

8) Unless you have purchased a new car or home in the last 12 months, the chances of your seeing a credit report are 1in 8.

9). Over 90% of Americans have no idea what their rights are under "Federal" and "State" credit and collections laws.

10). Only 1 in 20 Americans has a current listing on file, of all credit card accounts including numbers to refer to in the event of theft or fraud.

TRAINING MATERIAL

Position title: Collector
Department: Collection Department

GENERAL SUMMARY:

Work on behalf of (collection agency name) and their clients to recover debt. Initiate contact with debtors and effectively communicate the importance of payment. Accurately researches account and establish leverage. Provide solutions to debtor and assist with structuring payment plans. When necessary recommend legal action.

ESSENTIAL JOB FUNCTIONS:

Research and analyze accounts prior to initiating debtor contact, examine historical data and evaluate past collection efforts.

Determine the most effective and economical means of collection for each account and apply standard due diligence to collect monies due.

Initiate contact within 24 hours of new business being entered into system.

Maintain complete records on all accounts including, but not limited to detailed documentation on all collection efforts.

Utilize available resources and skip tracing techniques to locate debtors and any relevant credit information pertaining to the individual responsible for the debt.

Advise debtor of proper payment schedules and the principles of credit and credit standings.

Maintain a consistent level of professionalism with the debtors at all times.

Generate correspondence through the use of system letters.

Follow company procedures at all times without exception.

Maintain organized and current physical files for open accounts in queue.

After 6 months of collection efforts, decide whether to litigate or close file.

Other various duties at the discretion of direct management.

KNOWLEDGE, SKILLS AND ABILITIES:

Knowledge of rules and regulations pertaining to collection methods and techniques.

Extensive knowledge of FDCPA and FCRA regulations.

Ability to read, write and comprehend abbreviated correspondence, memos and invoices.

Effectively communicate to debtors, support staff and management.

Ability to deal with problems involving a few concrete variables in standardized situations.

PERFORMANCE STANDARDS:

Achieve monthly goals

Work all queues accounts in a timely manner. Queue aging should not fall behind more than 60 days.

Handle all incoming and outgoing correspondence within 48 hours of receipt.

All duties are to be preformed in accordance with federal and state laws and presented in a professional manner.

Education and Experience

Six months to one year of previous experience.

Formal training in the collections industry and FDCPA regulations.

The statements herein are intended to describe the general nature and level of work preformed by employees assigned to this classification. They are not intended to be construed, as an extensive list of all responsibilities, duties and skills requires for personnel so classified.

TRAINING MATERIAL

HOW TO MAKE A DEMAND

"NEVER" IDENTIFY WITH A DEBTORS SITUATION:
If you identify with a debtor's situation, you become their friend and
thus losing the control needed to successfully collect the debt.

"NEVER" BECOME FRIENDLY WITH THE DEBTOR:
See answer above.

"NEVER" PREJUDGE A DEBTORS ABILITY TO PAY IN FULL
TODAY:
If you judge a debtor by his physical characteristics rather than his
financial ability, you will never be successful.

"NEVER USE THE PHRASES "can you", "will you", or "when can
you":
The debtor will almost always answer "NO" to these questions, never
give the debtor a way out of paying in full today.

"ALWAYS" BE PROFESSIONAL:
In doing so you will almost always stay in control of the conversation
between you and the debtor.

"ALWAYS" CONFIRM A PROMISE FOR PAYMENT:
By repeating what the debtor is saying, you confirm the arrangements
and take a psychological advantage by displaying you are in control of
the conversation.

"ALWAYS" FOLLOW UP ON BROKEN PROMISES
IMMEDIATELY:
Therefore the debtor has no other choice than to communicate why
they did not pay on time.

"ALWAYS" USE THE PHRASES "I suggest", "you need", or "you must":
By doing so you tell the debtor what is expected and leaves little room for them to get control of the situation.

Always keep your demand short and to the point, state your name, company name, whom your client is and the amount the debtor owes – then wait for a response.
After making your demand stop talking. **DO NOT** speak again until the debtor responds. Do not let the silence make you nervous, the first person to speak gives up control of the conversation.

EXAMPLE
My name is (your name) and I'm with (company's name), we represent (clients name) regarding an unpaid balance of (dollar amount) that is due today. You need to get your checkbook so you can pay this account over the phone with us today.
The debtor at this point will most likely have an excuse for non-payment. No matter what the excuse, you will almost always use the following comeback – **"I understand, however…"**

THE MAIN KEYS TO SPEAKING WITH DEBTORS:

Do not interrupt while the debtor is talking, be a good listener. In most cases the debtor is telling you what you need to do or say to get them to pay the bill.

Stay calm, do not raise your voice or argue, and never let the debtor push your buttons.
Always repeat what the debtor is saying when talking about a payment arrangement.

Always try to offer solutions for payment: (payment arrangement, credit card, electronic check, etc.).

Do not use dialog that suggest any type of legal action unless you intend to have a lawsuit filed.

When receiving a call from an irate or inconsiderate debtor, notify them to calm down or you will terminate the call. If they calm down and decide to discuss the account, proceed accordingly. If they continue to argue, use profanity or show no willingness to calm down, then terminate the call and decide if you should develop the account for a possible lawsuit. In most cases this type of debtor will not pay voluntarily.

Always remember, the collection process is not an emotional experience. Most of the time when the debtor is upset, they are not mad at you, but themselves for allowing their account to be placed with a collection agency.

NINE TIPS FOR SUCCESSFUL COLLECTIONS

6. **PREPARE:** Review the account and get an idea of what to say to the debtor before making the call.

7. **ATTITUDE:** Adopt a straightforward, professional business-like attitude. Our client provided services and now money is owed; we have a right to expect payment. Never let it become personal. Do not yell, raise your voice or make false threats and never swear. Remember that all debtors' can pay in full today if properly motivated.

8. **CONTACT:** Make sure your talking to the right person. Don't let the individual brush you off with an excuse *like "I'm too busy to talk right now."* If after leaving several messages and there is still no response, extend the account review date for 2 weeks and try again later or refer it to another collector for follow-up. When leaving messages on voice-mail try to rotate the times of the day you place your call and stay consistent until you make contact.

9. **CONTROL:** Always control the conversation. Keep focused on the debt and on the re-payment schedule. Do not let the debtor

sidetrack you with personal history, excuses, or personal stories. Remember, the **object of your call is to collect money** that is owed to our clients, not become buddies with the debtor or win arguments.

10. **FLEXIBLE:** Be ready to adjust to any situation. Think about the kind of debtor you are dealing with and adapt to meet the circumstances. Be prepared to accept a *reasonable* payment schedule, and willingness to deal with a debtor's circumstances.

11. **NOTES:** Keep detailed and accurate notes on every account. This will help you when making subsequent phone calls and may be invaluable if we have to litigate the account.

12. **PRODUCTIVITY:** Keep contact brief and to the point. This is a business call and not a social one. View your efforts on a ratio of **time expended** to **results achieved.** Long conversations usually mean the debtor is stalling you, or trapping you in the buddy syndrome.

13. **PRECISION:** Never leave a contact open ended, such as *"we'll talk next week,"* or *"I'll see what I can do for you and call you back."* Every contact should result in a commitment of payment of a specific amount by a specific date.

14. **TIME:** The longer we have an account, the less likely it will become profitable. Remember, we don't get paid unless we collect. Therefore, it is important to work all accounts within a **consistent** time frame from initial contact to finality.

THE IMPORTANCE OF DEADLINES

Always give the debtor a deadline. The purpose of this is to give the debtor the perception that there is a sense of urgency in getting the bill paid quickly and without their timely cooperation they can only blame themselves for any further collection activity that maybe taken.

HOW DO WE DO THIS?

During your initial demand for the full payment, explain to the debtor that they have until a specific date of any given month to come up with payment in full. Under any circumstances do not allow the debtor to make an arrangement for the last day of the month. Always give yourself a minimum of 2 days of leeway to ensure you have the opportunity to still work something out for that month. Then, within a day or two of the due date, call the debtor and reinforce or confirm the arrangements you made previously. If the debtor responds negatively and claims he cannot make the payment as agreed, you must use your flexibility and convince the debtor he has to come up with some kind of payment or you will not be able to help him. Once a payment arrangement has been reached, make sure you explain to them that it is important to have the payment in our office no later than the agreed upon date. Remember to always repeat due dates and dollar amounts and have the debtor sign a promissory note if necessary.

What to do when dealing with a debtor whose payment arrangement falls past due 30 days or more on a consistent basis:

Notify the debtor that their account is in default and the balance is due in full today. They will most likely want to argue with you as they probably cannot or do not have payment in full.
Inform the debtor that you can help them but they need to get their account caught up plus one extra payment to show good faith and their desire to pay the account in full as soon as possible.
If the debtor agrees to catch up their payments, always try to get their permission to set them up on a post-dated electronic check agreement.

EXAMPLES:

"You must make your payment to our office by 4pm Thursday or I may not be able to help you further."

"If you cannot come up with the full balance, then I can probably give you a 15 or 30-day extension. However, you must have at least $300 by 4pm Thursday."

"I am calling to inform you that your arrangements with our office regarding your account is more than 30 days past due. Because of this the entire balance is due in our office no later than 4pm Thursday." Remember; do not argue with the debtor – you are simply making a courtesy call.

End of training material

COLLECTION AGENCY MYTHS

Myth: A collector will come to your door to collect.
Fact: the media has perpetuated the image of a collector knocking on your door for years. In reality collectors rarely go to anyone's home or business to collect. Using telephones in combination with modern technology, today's collector can make hundreds of contacts a day more so than by going door-to-door.

Myth: Collection agencies will file suit for any amount.
Fact: No, most agencies will only file suits against consumers when the debt is at least $500 or more. In some cases, some agencies will go as low as $300, and they cannot file suit if you live in a different state than them.

Myth: Collection agencies force people into bankruptcy.
Fact: in reality it does not make sense for a collector to encourage a consumer to file for bankruptcy. Collectors are trained to understand that people in financial trouble often need guidance in settling their accounts without expensive litigation. A collector's business is to collect, but in practice, collecting often includes counseling

Myth: Collectors hassle people who cannot pay.
Fact: one of the first lessons a collector learns is that constant harassment of a consumer is both ineffective and illegal under the Fair Debt Collection Practices Act (FDCPA). Instead collectors are trained to listen to what consumers say and determine if they actually have the resources to pay the past-due bill.

Myth: Collection agencies can call your neighbor.
Fact: Yes, however, they cannot disclose the nature of their call nor can they disclose whom they work for.

Myth: A Collector is a rare breed of people.
Fact: Collectors come from all backgrounds with different experiences. They tend to be quick thinking, goal oriented, problem solving and effective communicators.

Myth: Collection agencies misrepresent themselves.
Fact: No, it is illegal and immoral and a very big no-no. If an agency is caught misrepresenting themselves, it could cost them their business and effectively shut them down.

Myth: Tough, threatening collectors are the most effective.
Fact: the most effective collectors are well-trained, sophisticated professionals who understand what motivates people and can determine quickly what will motivate a particular person and are able to communicate well with others. The best collectors work with people to get their accounts paid.

Questions and Answers

If you use credit cards, owe money on a personal loan, or are paying on a home mortgage, you are a "debtor." If you fall behind in repaying your creditors, or an error is made on your accounts, you may be contacted by a "debt collector." You should know that in either situation the Fair Debt Collection Practices Act requires that debt collectors treat you fairly and prohibits certain methods of debt collection. Of course, the law does not erase any legitimate debt you owe.

Why are accounts assigned to collection agencies?
Accounts are referred to collection agencies because they are in a past due or default status and the original creditor has not received any satisfactory communication from the consumer. Since third party collection agencies use specialized telephone systems, computers and software designed specifically for the collection industry, they are more effective then credit grantors at collecting payment on delinquent accounts.

What debts are covered under the Fair Debt Collection Practices Act?
Personal, family and household debts are covered under the act. This includes money owed for the purchase of an automobile, medical care or for charge accounts.

Who is a debt collector?
A debt collector is any person who regularly collects debts owed to others. This includes attorneys who collect debts on a regular basis.

How may a debt collector contact you?
A collector may contact you in person, by mail, telephone, telegram or fax. However, a debt collector may not contact you at inconvenient times or places, such as before 8am or after 9pm, unless you agree. A debt collector also may not contact you at your place of employment if the collector knows that your employer disapproves of such contacts.

Can you stop a debt collector from contacting you?

You can stop a debt collector from contacting you by writing a letter to the collector telling them to stop. Once the collector receives your letter, they may not contact you again except to say there will be no further contact or to notify you that the debt collector or the creditor intends to take some specific action. However, please be advised that sending such a letter to a collector does not make the debt go away if you actually owe it.

May a debt collector contact anyone else about your debt?

If you have an attorney, the debt collector must contact the attorney rather than you. If you do not have an attorney a collector may contact other people, but only to find out where you live, what your phone number is, and where you work. Collectors usually are prohibited from contacting such third parties more than once. In most cases, the collector may not tell anyone other than your attorney or your spouse, depending on the law of the state you live in that you owe money.

What must the debt collector tell you about the debt?

Within 5 days after you are first contacted, the collector must send you a written notice telling you the amount of money you owe; the name of the creditor to whom you owe the money; and what action to take if you believe you do not owe the money.

May a debt collector continue to contact you if you believe you do not owe money?

A collector may not contact you if, within 30 days after you receive the written notice you send the collection agency a letter stating you do not owe money. However a collector can renew collection activities if you are sent proof of the debt, such as a copy of a bill for the amount owed.

What types of debt collection practices are prohibited?

Harassment – debt collectors may not harass, oppress, or abuse you or any third parties they contact. For example, debt collectors may not: Use threats of violence or harm

Publish a list of consumers, except to a credit bureau
Use obscene or profane language
Repeatedly use the telephone to annoy someone.

False statements – debt collectors may not use any false or misleading statements when collecting a debt. For example, a debt collector may not:

1. Falsely imply that they are attorneys, or government representatives.
2. Misrepresent the amount of your debt.
3. Falsely imply that you have committed a crime.
4. Falsely represent that they operate or work for a credit bureau.
5. Indicate that the papers being sent to you are legal forms when they are not.
6. Indicate that papers being sent to you are not legal forms when they are.

Debt collectors also may not state that:
You will be arrested if you do not pay your debt
They will seize, garnish, attach or sell your property or wages unless the collection agency intends to do so, and it is legal to do so
Actions such as a lawsuit will be taken against you when such action legally may not be taken or when they do not intend to take such action

Debt collectors may not:
Give false credit information about you to anyone, including a credit bureau
Send you anything that looks like an official document from a court or government agency when it is not.
Use several false names

Unfair practices – debt collectors may not engage in unfair practices when they try to collect a debt. For example, collectors may not:

Collect any amount greater than your debt, unless your state permits such a charge.

Deposit a post-dated check prematurely

Use deception to make you accept collect calls or pay for telegrams

Take or threaten to take your property unless this can be legally done

Contact you by postcard

What control do you have over payment of debts?

If you owe more than one debt, any payment you make must be applied to the debt you indicate. A debt collector may not apply a payment to any debt you believe you do not owe. However, if you do not indicate which account to apply the payment to, it will be applied to any balance you may owe, per the agency's directive.

What can you do if you believe a debt collector violated the law?

You have the right to sue a collector in state or federal court within one year from the date the law was violated. If you win, you may recover money for the damages you suffered plus an additional amount up to $1,000. Court costs and attorney fees also can be recovered. A group of people also may sue a debt collector and recover money for damages up to $500,000 or one percent of the collector's net worth, whichever is less.

Where can you report a debt collector for an alleged violation?

You can report any problems you have with a debt collector to your state Attorney General's office and the Federal Trade Commission. Many states have their own debt collection laws and your Attorney General's office can help you determine your rights. The Fair Debt Collection Practices Act (FDCPA) was enacted in 1977 to protect consumers from unfair or abusive collection practices. To file a complaint call toll free to 1-877-FTC-HELP or use the complaint form at www.ftc.gov.

THE FAIR DEBT COLLECTION PRACTICES ACT

LEARN EXACTLY WHAT EACH SECTION OF THE FDCPA REALLY MEANS.

Section 804 - Acquisition of location information

Meaning - A bill collector may contact your relative, neighbor or employer as long as he identifies himself by name but cannot disclose the name of his employer. He is not allowed to disclose in anyway that you owe money but that he is only confirming location information. Furthermore, he is allowed to contact a third party such as a neighbor or relative only once, unless they request that he call back or if the collector has a good reason to believe that they purposefully withheld information.

Section 805 - Communication in connection with debt collection

Meaning - A collector may only call you between the hours of 8:00 AM and 9:00PM within your time zone. Also, a collector may not contact you at your place of employment if he has reason to believe you are not allowed to take calls at work. Reason to believe can be established by telling the collector that you are not allowed personal calls at work.

Section 806 - Harassment or abuse

Meaning - A collector may never use obscene or otherwise abusive language towards you. Also, a collector may never attempt to embarrass you in any way.

Section 807 - False or misleading representations

Meaning - This section has various meanings - A collector may not use deceptive or misleading means in an effort to collect a debt. This could include the following:
Falsely implying that he is an attorney or government representative.
Falsely implying that you have committed a crime.

Representing correspondence as being from an attorney when it is not.

Implying that non-payment of any debt will result in loss of personal property, wages, or arrest unless the debt was incurred unlawfully or they intend to follow-thru with such action.

Threatening to take action that is not legal or that the collector does not intend to take.

The false representation that you committed a crime in an effort to disgrace you.

Misrepresenting your credit or failing to communicate that you are disputing a debt.

The use of written communication that simulates or is falsely represented to be a document authorized, issued or approved by any court, official or agency of the United States or any state, or which creates a false impression as to it's source, authorization or approval

The use of any false or deceptive means to attempt to collect a debt or obtain information about you. Failure to disclose clearly in all written communication that the collector is attempting to collect a debt and any information obtained will be used for that purpose.

Section 808 - Unfair Practices

Meaning - This section has various meanings:

1. A collector may not collect any interest, fees or collection charges unless it is legal or if it was expressly authorized in the original agreement that created the debt.

2. If a collector accepts a check that is more than 5 days postdated, he must notify you in writing a minimum of 3 days and a maximum of 10days before depositing your check.

3. A collector may not solicit a postdated check for the purpose of threatening or instituting criminal prosecution.

4. A collector may not deposit or threaten to deposit a post-dated check before its intended date.

5. A collector may not cause charges to be incurred by you for the sake of communication such as a collect phone call or telegram fees.

6. A collector may not threaten non-judicial action to take property if there is no right to the property or if he does not

intend to take such action or the property is exempt from such action.

7. A collector may not use any means of mail that might be embarrassing to you such as a postcard or an envelope with a symbol or wording that indicates that it is a debt collection letter. He may use his business name on the envelope if it doesn't indicate that it is a debt collection business.

8. A collector may never give false credit information about you to anyone.

Section 809 - Validation of debts

Meaning - A debt collection agency must notify you in writing within 5 days of the initial communication of the following:

1. The amount of the debt.
2. To whom the debt is owed.
3. A 30-day right to dispute the account. (Failure to dispute the account within 30 days will not be construed by any court to mean an admission of liability).

Section 810 – Multiple Debts

Meaning - If you owe more than one debt to the same collection agency, all payments must be credited to the account(s) as instructed by you. A collection agency may not apply a payment to one debt if it was clearly intended for another; nor may your payment be applied to an account that is currently being disputed.

Section 811 - Legal actions by debt collectors

Meaning - If a collection agency takes legal action against you, they must do so where the mortgaged property is located, where you live or where you signed the contract. In other words, a collection agency in Arizona can't file action against you in an Arizona court if you live in or signed the contract in California.

Well, that's pretty much it - Now, if you think you have been treated unfairly by an abusive bill collector, you should consult with your attorney to determine if you have sufficient grounds for filing a lawsuit. Public Law 95-109 does provide guideline for a civil liability suit up to $1,000 within one year of the actual incident. However, state laws can add restrictions placed on collection agencies attempting to collect a debt, but they cannot annul or reduce any of the requirements outlined in public law 95-109. You can receive additional information by contacting your state Attorney General's office. If you have been harassed but do not want to or are not ready to pursue legal action, you should at the very least report the incident to the Federal Trade Commission or what is also known as the FTC and your state Attorney General's office. The FTC National Headquarters can be contacted at:

FTC
2121 "L" Street NW
Washington, DC 20530
(202) 326-2222

THE FAIR CREDIT REPORTING ACT

LEARN EXACTLY WHAT EACH SECTION OF THE FCRA REALLY MEANS.

604 - Permissible Purposes of Reports

Meaning - Your credit report may be requested by those who have a legitimate business need for the information. This would include for purpose of granting credit, providing insurance and employment. You have the right to have your file withheld from those you have not given a real business need for requesting it.

605 - Obsolete Information

Meaning - Negative information must be removed from your file after 7 years from the time it was reported. The major exception is bankruptcy or other listings of public records such as judgments.

606 - Disclosure of Investigative Consumer Reports

Meaning - A company must send you notice that they are conducting an investigative consumer report within 3 days from the time they request such a report. You have the right to then request from that company more information as to the nature and scope of the investigation.

607 - Compliance Procedures

Meaning - Requires the credit-reporting agency to follow reasonable procedures to assure maximum possible accuracy of any information contained in your report. Information contained in a report must be accurate and pertain to the individual as to what is being reported.

608 - Disclosure to Governmental Agencies

Meaning - A consumer reporting agency may furnish identifying consumer information limited to your name, address, former addresses, places of employment or former places of employment to a government agency.

609 - Disclosures to Consumers

Meaning - Upon request, a credit-reporting agency must reveal the nature, substance and sources of the information collected about you.

610 - Conditions of Disclosure to Consumers

Meaning - You have the right to take anyone such as an attorney, accountant, etc. with you to the credit bureau when you view your file.

611 - Procedure in Case of Disputed Accuracy

Meaning - You may dispute anything in your file that is inaccurate. The bureau has 30 days to verify the information with the original source, or it must be removed. If the information is confirmed by the source that reported it, but you still believe it to be inaccurate, you may have a statement of up to 100 words added to your file explaining the circumstances surrounding that item. You can then request that your statement be sent to any company that received your file without your side of the story. If the information is found to be incorrect and thus removed, at your request the bureau must make notification of the correction to any company that received the wrong information. There can be no charge to you for them to do this.

612 - Charges for certain Disclosures

Meaning - You may request free of charge all information to which you are entitled if the request is made within 60 days after receipt of a notification that you have been denied credit, insurance or employment because of information contained in your report. Otherwise the credit reporting agency is permitted to charge a fee established by the FTC. The charge in most states is $8.

613 - Public Record Information for Employment Purposes

Meaning - Requires the credit-reporting agency to notify you that information of public record is being reported and that the information being reported is complete and up to date.

614 - Restrictions on Investigative Consumer Reports

Meaning - All information being reported by a credit reporting agency must be verified before it can be added to a consumer report.

615 - Requirements on Users of Consumer Reports

Meaning - A company who denies you credit, insurance, employment or raises the cost of your insurance or credit due to information obtained from a credit reporting agency must inform you which agency the negative information came from.

616 - Civil Liability for Willful Noncompliance

Meaning - Any person or company that willfully fails to comply with any requirement imposed under this title, is liable for an amount equal to actual damages sustained by you or damages of not less than $100 and not more than $1,000. Any person or company who obtains a consumer report under false pretenses or knowingly without permission is liable for actual damages sustained by you or $1,000 whichever is greater. Plus you are entitled to punitive damages, and any costs of the action as the court may allow.

617 - Civil Liability for Negligent Noncompliance

Meaning - You have the right to sue a credit reporting agency for damages if the agency willfully or negligently violates the law; and, if you are successful, to collect attorney's fees and court costs.

618 - Jurisdiction of Courts; Limitation of Actions

Meaning - An action to enforce any liability created under this title may be brought in any appropriate United Stated district court with competent jurisdiction, within 2 years from the date the liability occurred or anytime within 2 years after the discovery of the misrepresentation.

619 - Obtaining Information Under False Pretenses

Meaning - Any person who knowingly and willfully obtains information on a consumer from a credit reporting agency under false pretenses is subject to be fined under title 18 of the United States Code, imprisoned for not more than 2 years, or both.

620 - Unauthorized Disclosures by Officers or Employees
Meaning - Any officer or employee of a credit reporting agency that knowingly and willfully provides information of a consumer from the agency's files to a person not authorized to receive that information shall be fined under title 18 of the United States Code, imprisoned for not more than 2 years or both.

621 - Administrative Enforcement
Meaning - Definition is not available - please see information on page 96

622 - Information on Overdue Child Support Obligations
Meaning - In accordance with section 604 of this title, any credit reporting agency can include any information of the failure of the consumer to pay overdue child support obligations for not more than 7 years.

623 - Responsibilities of Furnishers of Information to Consumer Reporting Agencies
Meaning - Forbids creditors from reporting information they know is not accurate or knowingly contains errors.

Remember, the reason a collection agency is in business is to make money. The way they make money is quite simple. A creditor who is owed money by a consumer assigns an account to the collection agency. The agency in turn charges the creditor up to 50% of whatever they collect Plus, if the agency charges interest to the consumer, which in most states is acceptable by law, they get to keep that too. See the example below:

Amount assigned:................... $1000.00
Agency fee @ 40%: $400.00
Amount of interest: $46.17
Amount collected: $1046.17
Amount agency keeps:............. $446.17

The collector, who is the person you paid over the phone or mailed your payment to, will usually get anywhere from 10% to 25% of the amount collected. In this case the collector would receive approximately $44.62 to $111.55. This is why bill collectors are finely tuned money making machines. Imagine, if they collect $60,000 a month, the agency will make approximately $24,000 and pay the collector approximately $4800 to $6000 a month. This is why they are trained to always focus on the money you owe and never, ever identify with any of your personal problems. They're trained to give you the perception that they're only trying to help you, but what they're really trying to do is separate you from your money. They're trained on how to speak, what to say and how to close the deal. They're trained on how to get asset information and make it seem like everyday conversation. They're trained on how to negotiate, how to locate asset information without your help, and even how to get you to pay your bill involuntarily.

Their initial demand for payment will almost always be for payment in full.

They'll tell you that a payment arrangement at this time is not available. They'll tell you to try to borrow the money or see how much you can come up with by the end of the month. The purpose for this is because in most cases, if you're motivated correctly you will do everything you can to find the money and pay the account in full. However, if you can't come up with all of the money that's okay as you'll probably have come up with a larger amount than some small payment. The more you pay, the more they make.

Collectors are trained in various aspects of the human psyche. They know how to talk, what to say and when to say it. One of the things they are taught is how to identify what type of debtor you are. There are 5 different types of debtor. *The stall* – this debtor will pay eventually but will give every excuse in the world why he can't pay until he is motivated to do so.

The hardship case – this type of debtor in most cases really does not have the funds to pay the bill.
The credit criminal – as the name implies this is a debtor who is a professional deadbeat and will do anything to keep from paying the debt.
The poor budgeters – this is the type of debtor that has the money to pay but would rather spend it on other things.
The dispute – this type of debtor may have a legitimate grievance or may just be making excuses.

Once a collector has determined what type of debtor you are, their next step is to determine what it is they will have to say or do to get you to pay the bill. That's where good solid training comes into play. Most collectors will go through a basic training session before they are allowed to make even one call. They are taught to always stay focused on the money and how to get around your excuse for not paying right now.
The first thing they are taught is what methods do not collect money. They're taught to be creative and always give the perception that they are on your side and want to work with you. They know that they can never allow you to push their buttons because if they do they will lose control of the conversation and quite possible lose out financially. They know for an example that if they can at least get some sort of promise to pay or commitment to pay from you that they now have the advantage

which enables them to make quicker decisions as to whether or not you will pay and if they need to send the account to their attorney for a possible lawsuit. **Therefore, whatever you do – <u>do not</u> make a promise to a collection agency that you know you can't keep.**

WHAT TO DO, WHAT NOT TO DO

That brings us to what you should always do and what not to do when dealing with bill collectors:

15. Never call while you are upset. Arguing with a bill collector will not result in resolving your problem. It will only entice them to take a stand and not work with you in a manner that will help you get the results you are looking for and it quite possibly will get you sued.

16. Always stay calm, remember the old saying, you get more bees with honey than you do with vinegar. With that said, understand that the collector can work with you or against you. So always try to get them to understand your situation thus giving you an opportunity to get what you want.

17. Never talk to a debt collector in a tone that assumes they are stupid or inept or that you know more about your rights than they do. This, again, will only entice them not to help you, which will result in a lack of cooperation.

18. Always treat the collector with respect and ask intelligent questions

YOUR FIRST COLLECTION NOTICE

So, you've received a collection notice. **Don't panic**, everything is going to be okay. The first thing you will want to do is request validation of the debt (see letter Dispute/validation Request). Even if you know that you owe the debt, you should always request it. The reason why is because your rights under the FDCPA says you are entitled to request this information and that the collection agency must provide it within a reasonable amount of time. If the collection agency cannot validate your debt, they are not allowed to continue their efforts to collect it. However, once they validate the debt they will continue to use whatever action is necessary under the laws that govern them to collect the debt. So be prepared to have to pay it.

If you receive a collection notice and you realize you owe the debt but just forgot to pay it, before contacting the collection agency the first thing you will do is contact the original creditor. The reason you want to do this is because the original creditor will most likely take your payment without the added interest or collection charge the collection agency will add and there is a very good chance the account won't affect your credit report negatively. Therefore, contact the original creditor and make your arrangements, however, make sure you are prepared to pay the account in full. Once you have made the necessary arrangements, you will need to backdate your check to a date prior to the date on your collection notice and then mail it to the original creditor. Whatever you do, do not inform your original creditor that you received a collection notice. There are two reasons you should backdate your check. First, if your check indicates the bill was paid prior to the date it was assigned to the collection agency, the collection agency cannot charge you interest or a collection charge and will have to cancel your account and send it back to their client, therefore it won't ruin your credit. Secondly, because once your check has been cashed by the original creditor it becomes a legally tendered document which indicates you paid your account prior to it being assigned to the collection agency. Once the check is cashed make sure you send a copy of it to the collection agency showing them that the account has been paid, and was paid prior to it being sent to collections. Thus, making the collection agency cancel the account and return it to the original creditor, which will save you money and your credit rating.

If you contact the original creditor and they advise you that you need to contact the collection agency, don't panic. You still have other options available to you. Remember, if all you want to do is pay the debt, you have 30 days after receiving your collection notice to do just that without it affecting your credit rating. Contact the agency, notify the collector that you will pay them in full but before you do, they need to provide you with a letter indicating that your account will not be reported to any of the credit reporting bureaus. If they refuse to cooperate, you should contact the original creditor and notify them that the agency is refusing to cooperate and that all you want to is pay the account. Insist on sending the payment to them. When they agree, again backdate your check and follow the steps already discussed. The original creditor will cash your check and report the payment to the collection agency. Again, you are now in a position to protect your credit rating and you might save a few dollars as well. However, if there is no way around it and you have to deal with the collection agency you're still okay. If your intentions are to pay the account in full, simply restrict the back of your check to say that *"upon receipt of your payment the collection agency agrees to have any negative information that has been reported, immediately be deleted"*. If the collector you are dealing with seems unreasonable and won't cooperate you will need to talk to his or her supervisor. Stay calm, never use profanity or threaten anyone in anyway. Request to speak to the supervisor of the collection department. Once you have been transferred, find out the name of the person you are speaking with. In some cases, the individual you are talking to is just another collector pretending to be the supervisor. So make sure you get their title as well. If they refuse to give you any of this information, hang up and call the main telephone number for the agency. When the receptionist answers, ask him / her what the name of the collection manager is and ask to speak to them. Once you feel confident that you're speaking to the right person, explain why you are calling and that you are simply trying to resolve this account. Do not insult them in anyway or lecture them about how they should do their job, remember you are not their customer you are their inventory.

If you end up having to pay the collection agency, try to negotiate whatever interest they have added, as it is always negotiable. Start off as low as 20% to 25% and work your way up. They will tell you that they cannot negotiate and it is possible that the person you are speaking to does not have the authority to write-off the interest as there maybe a company policy in place preventing interest negotiation by anyone other than a supervisor. Therefore, if that is the case, get the supervisor on the phone and see what you can get done. Whatever you do, always, make sure that whatever arrangements you make they are put into writing by the collection agency on their letterhead.

Disputing the Debt

Contrary to popular belief, you cannot terminate or what is otherwise known as "firing" a collection agency (see letter "do not send this letter" on page 48). The collection agency does not work for you; they work for themselves on behalf of their client. Also, sending a letter that states you dispute the validity of your debt without explaining the nature of your dispute does not qualify your account as being disputed. The only way to legitimately dispute a debt is if the product or service was not received, was inadequate or defective or there is a discrepancy with the balance owed. If it is a medical bill, and you're insurance company was supposed to pay it but didn't, does not qualify as a disputed account as you are responsible for your own insurance company.

If you have a legitimate dispute – you will write a letter to the collection agency requesting validation of the debt and the nature of your dispute. Anytime you are sending information to a collection agency, you should do so via certified mail return receipt requested. Once the agency receives your letter they will notify their client as to the nature of your dispute and see if they can validate your account or if it is actually legitimate. If your dispute comes back as legitimate the agency will place the account in a dispute status to ensure that they do not mistakenly report it to any of the credit reporting agencies.

If your dispute is not legitimate - and comes back as a valid debt, the collection agency will notify you that the debt is owed and will proceed with their efforts to collect the amount owed, so be prepared to pay the account or show proof that you do have a valid dispute.

REQUESTING A PAYMENT ARRANGEMENT

Collectors are trained to always demand payment in full prior to accepting a payment arrangement from you. When you tell a collector that you cannot afford to pay the account in full, they will tell you that the opportunity to make payments is no longer available. They will suggest that you attempt to borrow the money from a friend or family member and make monthly payments to them or they will inform you that you can put the amount owed on a credit card and pay your credit card bank monthly.

If you persist the collector will most likely suggest that you take a couple of days and see what you can scrape up. They will give you a deadline as to when to call them back and hope that you call back with at least ½ of what you owe. Whatever you do, **do not make any promises you know you cannot keep**. A good collector will be able to determine if you can come up with the full payment or if a payment arrangement is necessary by asking just a couple of key questions. So whatever you do, do not give up any information that might indicate you can afford to pay in full. Always tell them that you rent your home because being a homeowner is considered a good asset and will most likely blow any chance you had of making a payment arrangement. If they ask you for your employment, tell them that you are a sub-contractor or self-employed. Why? – Because if you tell them where you work and exactly how much you make, then miss a payment, they will most likely have a lawsuit filed against you, then when they receive a judgment, they can easily garnish your wages, If you're self-employed or a sub-contractor it is a great deal harder for the agency to garnish your wages. If they ask you for your checking or savings information, tell them you do not have one. Once again, you need to be able to protect yourself. If the collector does not have this information they can't or won't request a lawsuit and if your story sounds good enough, you might qualify for a payment arrangement. Also, always remember, under no circumstances should you ever pay by personal check. Always protect yourself and your assets. Below I have included a couple of excerpts from a training manual that I created for one of the agencies I worked with. It should give you an idea of what factors they use to determine payment arrangements.

TRAINING MATERIAL

PAYMENT IN FULL

Always demand payment in full prior to accepting payment arrangements from all debtors. When the debtor says they cannot afford to pay in full but can make monthly payments; your response should be to tell them that the opportunity for payments is no longer available. Suggest to them that they need to borrow the money from a friend or family member and make monthly payments to them. Or inform them that we accept Visa or MasterCard and if they have a credit card available we can accept payment over the phone right now and make payments to their credit card company. If the debtor insists on monthly payments make sure you get asset info and advise the debtor you will attempt to get the best arrangement possible. But do not make any guarantees under any circumstances.

IF THE DEBTOR HAS GOOD ASSETS

Explain to the debtor that with their current financial standing a payment arrangement would not be possible at this time. Suggest to them that they seek a loan from a financial institution. If the debtor attempts to get a loan and is denied then and only then will we discuss a payment arrangement. At this point the debtor would be willing to set-up a lucrative payment arrangement, so don't be shy...

IF THE DEBTOR HAS BAD ASSETS

If the debtor has bad assets or no assets then you should look at a possible payment plan. Remember to always stay in control and tell the debtor what they need to pay. If you cannot come to a reasonable agreement terminate the call and try again later. Do not accept a payment plan you feel is not appropriate... REMEMBER – YOU ARE IN CONTROL.

WHAT CONSTITUTES GOOD ASSETS

Homeowner
Multiple car owners

Good & current credit rating
Lucrative earnings with their employer
Checking or savings account
Stocks, Bonds or 401k Programs

PAYMENT ARRANGEMENTS

A rule of thumb to go by when deciding on monthly payments is as follows:

$300. - $500.   = $50 Minimum
$501. - $800.   = $75 Minimum
$801. - $1000. = $100 Minimum

You should always require at least ½ to 1/3 down... (I.e.: if an account is $900, you should try to get approx. $450 down and payments of no less than $50 monthly).

Any balances under $300 should be payment in full or split into no more than 3 equal payments.

When the debtor requests a payment arrangement the first thing you need to do is confirm what he is saying, " you would like a payment arrangement, is that correct?" after confirming with the debtor you need to request asset information, let the debtor know that you will be willing to try to get an appropriate payment arrangement approved, however, you need to get some financial information first.

NEVER DISCUSS THE MONEY UNTIL YOU HAVE THE ASSET INFORMATION FIRST.

Once you have received the asset information you need to advise the debtor of the down payment amount and the approx. Amount of each monthly payment. Always use your best discretion, as the debtor will almost always try to get the smallest payment possible...BE FIRM. Remember the money the debtor sends is your livelihood.

If the debtor refuses to give you financial information, inform them that you are only trying to help them resolve this debt and that our client requires this information in order to approve any payment plan. If the debtor still refuses to cooperate, again BE FIRM, let them know that without this information you cannot help them and would not be able to accept any payments they might send unless, of course it's payment in full. If for some reason you cannot get financial information, then you need to advise the debtor that your collection efforts will continue until the account is resolved, at this point either transfer the call to a supervisor or terminate the call. You should never be afraid not to accept a payment arrangement. Remember that you are in control and always tell the debtor what they need to pay... never beg for a payment.

End of training material

How to Avoid a Lawsuit

First, keep in mind that a collector can only *refer* your account to the legal department. They do not file the lawsuit against you. Plus, most collection agencies have policies in place to help determine what account might be a good suit verses one that is bad. A good lawsuit is one where the balance is at least $500 and the collection agency has located at least 1 good asset on you and the account is not in dispute. A bad one is an account that is under $500 and has no assets or is in dispute. Once the decision is made that a lawsuit is needed to secure the money owed to their client, the account is put into a legal review status and the process to determine if your account will make a good suit or a bad suit begins. The first step the collection agency will take is to locate and/or verify asset information. If assets are located and verified, the next step is to run a credit report to determine your credit worthiness. If they are unable to verify your assets or can't find any, they will return your account to the general population queue and attempt to put you on a payment arrangement. However, if everything is looking good, they will write up what is called a suit sheet, attach all corroborating documents and refer it to the legal department for further processing. **I have enclosed a page from one of the training manuals I created a few years back regarding lawsuits.**

However, the best way to avoid a lawsuit is to pay your bill. If you're short on cash, try to borrow the money. The last thing you want is to be sued. Unfortunately there are really no little tricks that will prevent you from being sued unless you file for bankruptcy relief or your account has a legitimate dispute.

TRAINING MATERIAL

Lawsuits are an essential element in the over-all collection process. There are times, for various reasons, when a collector is unable to obtain payment in full. This is when the request to file a lawsuit is viable and in some cases necessary. In addition, time-management and working the account correctly from the very first contact is vital to the success of this process. It is important that you get as much asset information from the debtor as possible to ensure a systematic ease when requesting lawsuits. In other words, You should develop a system within your daily timetable on a step by step basis so you can stay focused on collecting money rather than sitting around and waiting for credit reports. Below is a basic strategy:

As you make contact with the debtors determine if the account fits within the pre-set criteria for a lawsuit.

If not – review and consider what information you need to acquire in order for the account to fit with in the criteria for suit.

If it does – request a credit report, note the file and create a list of all accounts that may be possible lawsuits.

Once you receive the credit report, determine the debtor's credit worthiness.

If it's not good – consider what alternatives, you have to get the debtor to pay without being able to file a lawsuit.

If it is good – get happy, you're half way there – review the credit report for additional and verifiable asset information.

Verify asset information.

If asset information is non-verifiable – set the file aside until such a time can be afforded were the information can be verified or consider what alternatives are available to get the debtor to pay without filing a lawsuit.

If you obtain verification – write up the suit request sheet and note the computer file of all information and change status to **LRW** to indicate the account is in legal review.

Remember that lawsuits are money – as I said before, they are like a good retirement plan. The more work you do now the more residual income you will have later. National statistics show that on average, collectors file one suit per day for each working day of every month. That comes out to be about 240 suits per year. We have 100 collectors, which should give us about 24,000 suits a year. However, it costs money to file lawsuits. Therefore, we have adopted some stringent guidelines to help balance part of the costs attributed to suits that may be a waste of time or not worth the investment. However, as the suits come in and the training goes on – the guidelines will <u>relax</u>, it all depends on how many suits you request and at what level of consistency. The more accurate the information that you verify regarding assets, addresses and etc., the less work our legal staff has to do for you, and the quicker they will be able to file the suits.

End of training material

WHAT HAPPENS IF YOU DON'T PAY...?

Well, several things can happen. For instance, if the dollar amount owed is large enough a collection agency may refer your account to their attorney with the instructions to have a lawsuit filed against you. Plus your account will most likely be reported to at least one of the 3 major credit reporting agencies as an unpaid collection account which once listed on your credit report is considered a "bad" mark against you. What you have to understand is that you are responsible for your own debts. Here is an example:

You go to the doctor – which creates a bill – although you have insurance, and you gave your insurance information to the doctor, you are still responsible to pay the doctor as the services were rendered to you and not your insurance company. How do you handle this situation? Well first of all, you need to pay your account – get a copy of the bill along with a copy of the receipt and send it certified mail to your insurance company along with a 10-day demand letter for reimbursement. Your insurance company will reimburse you for the total amount you paid including any interest.

So, if you don't pay your bill and refuse to cooperate, you could be sued. If you are sued and the agency wins a judgment against you, you can expect to have your wages garnisheed, a lien filed against any real property you may own and a levy filed against any bank accounts you have. Plus, you can expect your bill to increase about 3 times the original amount you owe as the agency is entitled to recoup the money it spent having the lawsuit filed against you. Furthermore, you can also expect to have a public record of the judgment show up on your credit record for 10 years from the date the judgment was entered against you.

Here's a step-by-step look from start to finish:

1. After the account is assigned to a collection agency, the first thing a collector will do is check to see if you have any other accounts in their system.

2. Next, they will review any paperwork to determine if there is any miscellaneous information that may help them when making their demand.

3. Now, they call you either at your place of employment or home and make their demand. If you refuse to cooperate, they will follow the next several steps.

4. Requests a credit report to determine if you pay your other bills see if you own any property and to see if you have any credit cards that you could use to pay this account. Also, it could help locate a place of employment if needed.

5. Next, they will check with one of the many Internet database companies to verify your address so they know where to have you served with a summons and complaint.

6. Once they have verified your address, and checked your credit, the next thing is to verify what is known as an asset. An asset is anything of a material value, such as a job, a piece of property or a bank account.

7. Once they have located and verified an asset, all of the paperwork is submitted by the collector to the collection agency legal department.

8. When the legal department receives the information from the collector, a file is made and all necessary paperwork needed to have a suit filed against you is typed up.

9. Once all the necessary documents are ready and after the attorney has signed them, the legal department will then file the suit.

10. Once the suit is filed, the agency then has the county sheriff serve you with a summons and complaint, which is legal notice to you that you are being sued.

11. Once you've been served, you have anywhere from 20 to 30 days to file an answer, depending on what state and county you live in.

12. After the thirty days are up, the agency will immediately summons the court to rule in their favor — this is called a summary judgment.

Once they have their judgment - watch out - this is where it starts to get costly. First thing the agency will do is file for a writ of execution - this means they are now in the process of attempting to garnishee your wages, file a lien against any real property you may own and possible levy any money you may have in a checking, savings or money market account. In some states, once a collection agency has their judgment they can even force you to sell any real property you may own at auction and then take the proceeds.

HOW THEY FIND YOU

With today's technological advances, combined with the Internet, it's now easier than ever before for a collection agency to get the information they need to locate you and make demand for payment. Back in the good old days, before the Internet, it was much more difficult. Information wasn't as readily available as it is today. Now, there are literally thousands of companies and governmental agencies that keep databases with all kinds of information on you. Just remember, anytime you fill out a credit application, or apply for a job or even register to vote, you are updating and sending out current information about you that anyone can get.

How do collection agencies find you? It's pretty simple really; one of the first things a collection agency or bill collector will do is check any and all paperwork they received from their client and look for a possible place of employment, or maybe a nearest relative. If that doesn't work then the next step is to take the personal information they received from their client and forward it to one of the database companies so they can run it through their database and try to verify your information as either being correct or not correct. If that doesn't work, then the next step is to have a credit report run so they can check to see if you applied for credit recently. Remember, when you apply for credit - your credit report is automatically updated with whatever information you used on the credit application. However, even if you haven't applied for credit in a while, a credit report is still very valuable. The reason is it always lists the name, address and phone numbers of all the other creditors that are reporting to the credit bureau regarding your credit with them. A bill collector will call these other companies and try to get as much current information about you as they can. Also, a credit report lists your last known place of employment, who your spouse is if any, and any public record information you may have such as a judgment or tax lien. The next way a bill collector may get updated or new contact information is by calling your neighbors. Yes that's correct, they call the next-door neighbor from your last known address - How? Simple, believe it or not, there are actual information directories that anyone can purchase or lease that will give you telephone information by looking up an address, but also will give you an address by looking up the phone number. A smart bill collector will look up the phone numbers for your previous neighbors and give them a call. You would be amazed how much information a collector can get by using this technique.

How to Get a Collection Agency to Delete Your Account:

There are several ways this can be done. However, let me just say that if your looking for a quick fix – this isn't it.

Collection agencies are required to notify you by mail that an account has been assigned to them for collections. They are also required to allow you an opportunity to dispute your account within a reasonable amount of time once you have been notified of the debt. However, if you are never notified of the debt being assigned to them for collections, they cannot report it to the credit bureaus. Therefore, if you receive something in the mail that may look like a notice from a collection agency you may want to simply write across the front of the envelope "moved – not at this address" and drop it off in a public mailbox outside of your postal zip code. The reason you do not want to put it back in your own mailbox is because the postal worker who delivers your mail may think you have really moved and may not continue to deliver your other mail. If you drop it off in a public mailbox outside of your postal zip code area, the letter will go to a different post office and therefore the local post office that handles mail delivery to your address will not be notified that you may have moved and your other mail will continue to be delivered. Once the collection agency is notified that they have the wrong address, they will note your account of a "mail return" address and code your account accordingly. Thus, changing the status so the account information will not be reported to the credit bureaus. However, in some cases the information may have already been reported prior to them being notified that they have an incorrect address. In that case, when you are ready to pay the bill you will have to notify them that you were never notified of the debt and request that they delete the account information, as the law requires.

Another way to accomplish this feat is to dispute your account within the first 30 days of being notified of the debt being assigned to the collection agency. If you have a valid dispute, the collection agency cannot report the account as a valid collection account. However, if your dispute is not valid, the agency will report the information anyway.

Another way is to request proper validation of the debt, sort of. What you will do is write a series of letters that are backdated which looks as though you have been attempting to resolve your account and have continuously requested validation but the agency has never responded to any of your requests. Keep in mind that a collection agency must validate a debt or they cannot report to a credit bureau, or if they have already reported the information, they must have it deleted if they cannot validate the debt. See the sample letters starting on page 51 to get an idea of what I'm talking about.

HOW TO NEGOTIATE A SETTLEMENT AND SAVE YOURSELF UP TO 75% OF THE AMOUNT YOU OWE.

Collectors only have a certain amount of time to sue you for payments. The first thing you should do is determine if the statute of limitations for collecting a debt in your state have past. If the debt is older than the statute of limitations, you tell the bill collectors they are wasting their time by harassing you for an un-collectable debt, as the original creditor or the assigned collection agency cannot take you to court to get a judgment.

After 7 seven years (in most cases), a debt will disappear from your credit report. If the debt has gone unpaid for 7 years, then it can no longer legally remain on your credit report. You can challenge this listing on your credit report and it will come off. **Please note the amount of time a late payment can appear on your credit report has nothing to do with the statute of limitations.** Even though a debt may no longer legally appear on your credit report after 7 years, you could still be sued for the debt because the statute of limitations for your debt in your state is not up.

If the debt is gone from your credit report AND the statute of limitations is up on this debt, you're home free! If enough time has past for both the legal debt collection statutes of limitations *and* the credit report limitations have passed, don't worry about the debt! If your debt meets both of these conditions, it is un-collectable and it cannot appear on your credit report! If you get to this point, stop here, you are done!

My debts are not past the statute of limitations, and I need to settle them.

It is possible, but not guaranteed, of course, that the average consumer can settle a debt for about 75 cents on the dollar. You will be money ahead by doing this. However, your credit report may reflect the fact that you didn't pay as agreed, and future creditors will be more reluctant to grant you credit. We'll discuss ways to improve your chances of both settling your debts for less than what you owe and getting the negative information deleted from your credit report.

Understanding the True Risks and Realities of Overdue Debts

Most consumers overestimate the risk involved with overdue debts. They worry about possible repercussions such as wage garnishment and property seizure by their creditors. When the debt relates to a secured property, such as an automobile or a home, the possibility of repossession is quite serious. In the case of unsecured debts (such as credit cards) the dangers are much less serious.

It is important to remember, however, that the creditor would be within his rights to get a garnishment and seize property, even for a small debt. There is a risk of financial reprisals when any debt goes unpaid.

In fact, very few creditors will push all the way to a garnishment on a relatively small-unsecured debt for the simple reason is that creditors must obtain a judgment before doing this. Getting a judgment and subsequent garnishment and seizure are a creditor's most terrifying weapons in collecting past due debt, but they are expensive and time-consuming. Even if the creditor went all the way to recover the small debt, they probably wouldn't be able to recover enough to offset their collection costs. Therefore, there is very little risk of a creditor taking an unsecured debt farther than simple collections.

Many consumers fold under the perceived strain of unpaid debts. Hundreds of bankruptcies take place in the United States each week for amounts under $5,000. These consumers are so intimidated by their creditors that they flee to bankruptcy, even though bankruptcy can bring financial hardship if you don't do all the right things for the next ten years. If these same consumers had simply waited, ignoring the threatening letters and telephone calls, they would have realized that their creditors were all bark and no bite. Bankruptcy is the best option for some few consumers, but it is much overused. And, when a consumer files for bankruptcy, everyone loses -- especially the creditors.

The risks of judgments, garnishments, and property seizures must be properly balanced against the likelihood that such drastic collection measures will ever happen. The risk, and the decision to take that risk, is entirely yours if you're in such a position.

Debts that are Good Candidates for Settlement

Most unsecured debts can be settled. An unsecured debt is a debt where there is no collateral. Unsecured debts include medical bills, credit cards, department store cards, personal loans, collection accounts, student loans, amounts remaining after foreclosure or repossession, and bounced checks. There are very few creditors who will ever compromise; however most will take less-than-full amount owed as settlement if it will close a troublesome account. (Utility companies, however, rarely settle for less than the full balance.)

Secured debts (such as a home or automobile) are an entirely different story. If the creditor can simply repossess the property, why should he negotiate? You can often re-negotiate a short payment relief with a secured debt but don't attempt to settle the account while you still possess the property.

Also, the creditor must have a good reason to want to settle. If the account is paid current and there is no recent history of late payment, it will be difficult to convince the creditor that it is in their best interest to settle. (This should not be read, as recommendations to stop paying bills that are current. If you stop paying your current bills, you will almost certainly make your credit situation worse.) Perhaps bad credit is not an issue for you at this point and you feel you must stop paying your bills in order to settle them and get back on top of your debt load. If this is the case, you make that decision at your own risk. In other words, don't do it.

Tactics for Getting the Upper Hand

You have the natural advantage in debt settlement, because you have something the creditor wants. You must hold out for your terms until the creditor gives you what you want. Once you've written that settlement check, your advantage disappears.

Get your terms *in writing* before you even open your checkbook. *Never*

Expect a creditor to meet an agreement that was made verbally. *Everything* must be in writing and, even then, you will probably have to fight to make the creditor live up to his end of the bargain.

Keep good records. This can be the difference between a good and bad settlement. Don't expect them to remember you or what you agreed upon.

Send all correspondence via registered mail (about $2 a letter).

Keep a copy of every letter you send.

Include a self-addressed, stamped envelope with every letter. (Make it as easy as possible for them to contact you.)

If you call, keep a log of when you spoke to the agencies, and who. Ask for the name of the supervisor that is in charge of the person you spoke to, as the turnover rate at collection agencies is high.

Follow up all phone correspondence with a letter (registered, of course).

Penalties and extra interest should be your first targets in reducing the debt Maybe you don't have sufficient funds to repay a debt in full when a creditor demands payment. In many cases, much of the debt represents interest and penalties accrued while the consumer was unable to pay. It will be in the best interests of both parties to reach a reasonable arrangement for settlement. Most companies would be thrilled to get you to pay the original debt even without the extra penalties they add on and will usually be more agreeable to waive these fees.

Time is on your side. As time passes, the creditors will likely stop calling and the debt will be filed away for future attention. The longer the debt remains uncollected, the better your chances will be of getting a good settlement. Eventually, the creditor will consider the bad debt a loss in order to receive a corporate tax write-off. This does not necessarily mean that they won't pursue you for the debt. The corporation may then collect on the debt themselves, sell or assign the debt to a collection agency, press for a judgment and garnishment, or temporarily ignore the debt. The course of action chosen by the creditor will vary widely between corporations and debts.

If you're contacted by more than one collection agency for the same debt, it means that the original creditor has hired a secondary or even tertiary collection agency. This indicates that the original creditor and even the first collection agency have given up on you. A collection agency that agrees to take your debt at this time will insist the original creditor pay a generous fee (usually 50%-60% of what is owed). Many secondary and tertiary agencies will take 33-55 cents on the dollar. If the agency hasn't been able to reach you by phone but knows that you are receiving its letters, it may be willing to take even less.

Never look too eager to settle. Take plenty of time to reach an agreement. Don't accept the first, or even second, settlement offer. Make sure that they are the ones calling you to push the deal forward. You cannot expect to reach an affordable settlement if the creditor thinks he has the upper hand. If, for example, you tell a creditor that you really need to get this debt settled to get into your dream home; you can forget any kind of settlement. The creditor will insist on the full balance.

Remind the creditor that the statute of limitations is approaching on the debt and they only have a limited time to deal with you. Know when the statue is up on each debt and be prepared to give the creditor the time line.

Use the threat of bankruptcy. It will be in your best interest if the creditor believes that you have very little money and you are teetering on the edge of bankruptcy. You should approach each creditor as though this is their last chance to compromise, and get something out of your debt, before you declare bankruptcy and they get nothing. *Be careful when doing this, however.* If you accumulate any more debt after stating this to a creditor, (and they record all of your correspondence and phone calls), you may not be able to discharge this debt within bankruptcy.

Don't forget! Negotiate your credit rating with the creditor
The next thing you should do is negotiate your credit rating with the creditor. *This is very important* as a "paid" collection is negative to your credit rating as an "unpaid collection", making all your negotiation efforts and hard cold cash will do nothing to rebuild your credit report.

Negotiating your credit rating
You should always push for a Perfect Pay Rating. Your final goal in negotiating your credit rating is to get the creditor to list your credit rating after the settlement as "Paid as Agreed" or "Account Closed - Paid as Agreed". Anything other than this listing will have a negative effect on your credit report.

Creditors make their profits by collecting from their customers, not by reporting negative credit information. Because creditors recognize this "catch-22" situation, they will often agree to delete any negative listing upon settlement of the debt. You have to realize that creditors won't try to ruin your credit rating as a personal vendetta. It's strictly business. If it pays them to collect from you and restore your rating to perfect, they will do this. Talk to them in terms of money, not principals or morals. Something along the line of "I know you would love to receive the $3000 I owe you, but it will not help my credit report if you can't change my rating to 'Paid as Agreed'. All I have is $3000 and I will pay it to other creditors who will agree to change my credit rating in writing."

Collection agencies will always agree more readily to delete the negative listing than banks or credit cards. Why? They can change their rating, no problem, but you are still probably stuck with the original creditor reporting you late. And who cares if you have a "Paid As Agreed" collection account: no matter what the rating, *every collection account is a negative mark*. It's no skin off their nose to change it, and of no use to your credit.

You need to get the collection agency to agree to remove their listing entirely from your report and have the original creditor change the rating to "Paid As Agreed". At the very minimum, you are within your legal rights to demand the removal of the collection account from your report. The Fair Credit Reporting Act states that you cannot have more than one listing per delinquent account (meaning you can have the original creditor report you late but you **cannot** have a collection listed for this same account). If they refuse to remove their rating, tell them they are violating the Fair Credit Reporting Act which can lead to fines if don't remove the collection listing. Then report them.

Some collection agencies will tell you they have no power over what the original creditor will do regarding your credit. To some extent, this is true. However, both the collection agency and the creditor want their money. If collection agency gets paid, so does the creditor, therefore it is to their advantage to cooperate. And baloney if they tell you they don't know how to get a hold of the original creditor: did the account magically appear on the collector's desk? No. The collection agency was *hired*. Explain to the collection agency if they can get a written agreement from the creditor, you will pay them their money, or you will pay a more cooperative creditor with the only money you have left, and they get nothing.

Remember, though, not all collections result from credit cards. Doctor's bills and overdue utilities cannot appear on your report. But collections resulting from these accounts can. In the case of such collections, there is no duplicate negative listing, since the original creditor is not allowed to put a listing on your account, so this collection may legally remain on your report.

Many creditors, though, have an agreement with the credit bureaus that they will not allow a negative listing to be deleted upon settlement. While this is true, the creditor can just tell the credit bureau that they reported your rating inaccurately, not that it was due to settlement. Anything a creditor reports, a creditor can change. If this wasn't the case, creditors couldn't change erroneous information they may have placed on your account by mistake, and find themselves in trouble with the FTC. In most credit organizations, there are dozens of people with the authority to make changes on the credit report. Larger creditors, such as huge credit cards or banks will require you to apply more pressure before they will agree to delete a negative listing, but virtually every creditor will acquiesce with the right amount of persuasion.

The technical terms: Two approaches to having the negative information deleted upon settlement of a debt: pre-notification of terms and post-notification of terms.

Pre-notification of terms

You tell the creditor up-front that you will require the deletion of the entire negative listing as a term of the payoff. The agreement to delete the listing and consider the debt settled is documented in writing and signed before the payoff takes place.

Advantage: Time will be saved and you won't be disappointed at the last moment. It is also less likely that you will have to fight the creditor later to actually delete the negative listing.

Disadvantage: When the creditor discovers that your credit is important to you, he will usually ask for a larger settlement amount -- sometimes full balance -- to meet your terms.

Post-notification of terms: Once settlement negotiations are complete, the creditor receives the agreed payment along with an attachment to the check stating the requirement that the negative listing be deleted.

This approach requires use of a "conditional endorsement" document (drafted by your attorney) notifying the creditor of your terms.

Advantage: You will almost always get a better settlement amount. The creditor will often be tempted by the payoff when the terms arrive and will deposit the check without blinking at the new terms.

Disadvantage: The creditor may balk at the new terms, sending the settlement check back rather than cashing it. The creditor might still ask for more money or reject the deal altogether. If the creditor simply deposits the check without intending to follow through with your new terms, you will have to fight the creditor later and force him to delete the negative listing.

If you have to accept an imperfect credit listing as part of your settlement

You may find that some of your creditors are willing to hold out longer than you are before agreeing to delete the negative listing from your file. It may seem that they are unwilling to delete the negative listing under any circumstance. Once again, let it be said that every creditor will eventually give you what you want if you speak to the right person, are patient and persistent, and make the correct offer. But if you are on a time-line, and your attorney can't get them to agree to full deletion, you have a couple of other options:

List the account as "Paid" only. You may counter-offer that the creditors report the account as "Paid" rather than delete it altogether. This is a true indication of the status of the account and many creditors will concede and agree to this wording. A "Paid" status is still very negative for a collection account or an account that will show "Paid Charge-off" or "Paid Repossession." You should insist that the account show "Paid" *only* and that all other negative notations (such as "Charge-off," "Repossession," late notations, or "Collection") are deleted at the same time. A simple "Paid" notation on a regular trade line is neutral and should not hurt your credit.

List the account as "Settled" only. You may counter-offer that the creditors simply list the account as "Settled" rather than delete it altogether. "Settled" is an inherently negative listing but not as negative as "Paid Charge-off." Don't agree to a "Settled" listing until you have exhausted all other possibilities. "Settled" will still trigger a credit denial. You should only agree that the account show "Settled" if all other negative notations (such as "Charge-off", "Repossession", late notations, and "Collection") are deleted at the same time. If you agree to a "Settled" notation, you must continue to work hard to delete the notation through the credit bureau dispute process.

List the account as "Paid Charge-off" or "Paid Collection" or "Paid was 30-, 60-, or 90-days late." This will be the creditor's first choice, and your last choice, of what to place on your credit report once you have paid. These notations are almost as damaging as showing the same debt unpaid. It is very common, though, for an account to be deleted (through credit bureau disputes) once it has been paid. The creditor now has no compelling reason to keep the negative listing on your report. For this reason, it is still usually a good idea to settle even if the creditor won't budge on deleting or positively modifying the negative listing.

WHAT TO DO ONCE YOU HAVE SETTLED

NEVER DISCLOSE WHERE YOU WORK OR BANK.

If you are asked, simply say "no comment". The reason for this: If your settlement falls through, and the creditor gets a judgment against you, knowing where you bank or work will make it easy to collect the judgment.

NEVER PAY YOUR SETTLEMENTS WITH A PERSONAL CHECK

How you make payments is very important, as it protects you from other creditors learning about your financial status and bank account numbers. For this reason, never send a personal check. Get a cashier's check or money order. Make sure you get the money order or cashier's check from a different bank than your own bank or the post office.

MAKE SURE YOU KEEP A COPY OF YOUR MONEY ORDER OR CASHIER'S CHECK

Collection agencies keep notoriously bad records and it's your word against theirs if you say you paid and they said you didn't...unless you have the copy of the money order or cashier's check.

I NEGOTIATED A SETTLEMENT WITH A CREDITOR FOR LESS THAN I OWED. THE CREDITOR IS NOW SUING ME FOR THE BALANCE. IS THIS LEGAL?

Yes! You need to read the following information carefully.

Some collection agencies will agree to settle with you for far less than you owe and then turn around and hire another collection agency to collect the difference. However, in many states this is illegal. Once a creditor deposits or cashes a full payment check, even if she strikes out the words payment in full or writes, "I don't agree" on the check, she can't come after you for the balance. The states in which this law is enforced:

60

Arkansas	Colorado	Connecticut	Georgia	Kansas	Louisiana
Maine	Michigan	Nebraska	New Jersey	North Carolina	Oregon
Pennsylvania	Texas	Utah	Vermont	Virginia	Washington
Wyoming					

Some states have modified this rule. In the following states, if a creditor cashes a full payment check and explicitly retains his right to sue you by writing "under protest or without prejudice" with his endorsement, then he can come after you for the balance. But those exact words must be used. If he writes, "Without recourse, "communicates with you separately, notifies you verbally or writes on the check that it is partial payment, it is not enough.

Alabama	Delaware	Minnesota	Missouri	New Hampshire	New York
Rhode Island	South Dakota	Ohio	Wisconsin	Massachusetts	West Virginia

5 STEPS TO A BETTER CREDIT REPORT

Inaccurate reporting can be very costly. However, it=s never too late to get back on track. Bringing your credit worthiness back to a respectable level is not all that hard, just remember to stay consistent and patient.

ORDER YOUR CREDIT REPORTS.

First, contact the 3 credit bureaus and find out what each report has on it. There is a good chance that each one will be different, as not all creditors will report information to all three. Typically, your creditor will only subscribe to only one.

Equifax
PO Box 740241
Atlanta, GA 30374-0241
(800) 685-1111

Experian
PO Box 2104
Allen, TX 75013-0949
(888) 397-3742

Trans Union
760 W. Sprout Rd.
Springfield, PA 19064-4213
(800) 888-4213

If you have been denied credit in the last 60 days you are entitled to a free copy of your credit report. The company that checked your credit is required by law to supply you with the credit bureau=s name, address and telephone number. Simply notify the credit bureau that you have been denied credit and you are requesting your free copy.

EXAMINE YOUR REPORTS - CAREFULLY

You will probably find that there is at least one error on each of your credit reports. 7 out of every 10 consumers have inaccurate information listed on their reports. Your reports are generated by the credit bureaus from information that they receive from your creditors. They don=t verify it as being accurate or correct unless you request it. You will first want to look for everything from typing errors, outdated and incomplete information to inaccurate account histories. Make a thorough and meticulous list of items you dispute and the reasons why. If the negative information in our report is true and correct, only time can change that. That doesn't=t mean you can=t dispute it, but it will most likely be confirmed as being reported correctly and will remain on your report unchanged. Late payments and charge-off accounts will remain or your credit report for up to seven (7) years and bankruptcies and other matters of public records will remain up to ten (10) years. However, most potential creditors look for payment patterns rather than focusing one-time or rare occurrences, so on time and consistent bill payments will help improve your credit situation

DISPUTE - DISPUTE - DISPUTE

Remember a bad credit report can cost you, so be thorough. You can either complete the dispute form provided with your credit report or simply write a letter. Always clearly identify each inaccurate item and state the reason for your dispute.

Always keep copies of all records and forms plus the date the information was sent. The credit bureau must investigate any relevant dispute within 30days of receiving your letter. Any item that is not verified as accurate is removed. On occasion it will be necessary to contact your creditor to resolve the problem. If the credit bureau makes any changes to your credit file they will send you the results of their investigation along with a free updated copy of your report. Once an item has been removed, it cannot be put back on unless the creditor corrects the problem and sends you a written notice.

TIME TO NEGOTIATE

Now is the time to devise a spending plan that will reduce your debt and help you pay on time, every time. After your credit report comes back and if some items remain, it is time to contact your creditor and negotiate with them in an attempt to keep your accounts current and from being reported as delinquent. You will want to explain your current financial situation and ask for reduced monthly payments or change the due date in order to balance out your monthly bills.

The same strategy can be used for fixed-loan payments, but remember that this is only a short-term strategy. In most cases you will pay more interest to extend the repayment schedule, but it will allow you to stay current and save your credit rating. It=s important that you pay off each debt one at a time, gradually increasing payments to other debts.

Deal with collection accounts first as unpaid collection accounts are worse than a paid collection account. You can negotiate a pay-off settlement that may reduce your bill plus request that all derogatory remarks are removed from your credit report. Be sure to get all agreements in writing before sending our payment.

Next, you will need to slowly close out unneeded or unused credit accounts. Most experts recommend that you have no more than four major credit cards, depending on your income. But be careful when closing out these accounts as it can negatively impact your credit score. Your credit score is based on a ratio of total debts to total available credit. A good rule of thumb to go by is to keep your revolving debt to not more than your available credit. Remember, cutting the card in 2 and sending it back does not close out the account if there is a balance due.

ADD STABILITY TO YOUR CREDIT FILE

If you have ever been turned down for credit because of insufficient credit file, don=t despair, you can still add positive information to your credit file. Some creditors, such as gasoline card companies, local banks and credit unions may not report your credit history to the credit bureaus. You can attempt to ask the credit grantor to report your account information and monthly payment history to a credit-reporting agency. However, not all will do that. So, in the future, before opening a new account ask the potential credit grantor what their credit reporting policy is. If they don=t report account history then you may reconsider opening an account.

Now, if you have really bad credit, even a bankruptcy, don=t let your credit status go dormant. The faster you begin to re-establish good credit, the faster you can improve your credit score. It=s important to build a solid credit history. So, if you have bad credit one good place to start is with a secured credit card. There a many different offers out there, so search out the best deal you can find. However, limit the amount of times you apply for credit as credit bureaus report how many new accounts you have opened and the number of inquiries you have. The more inquiries and the amount of newly opened accounts can lower your credit score. Lastly, open a savings account at your bank. This will show potential credit grantors that you are working hard to save money and that you have reserves to repay your debt.

THE TEST

Below is a copy of a test most agencies require their new employees pass 100% before they can begin work.

FAIR DEBT COLLECTION PRACTICE ACT TEST

NAME_____   DATE_____

Write the "MINI MIRANDA" in its entirety.

THIS IS AN ATTEMPT TO COLLECT A DEBT AND ANY INFORMATION OBTAINED WILL BE USED FOR THAT PURPOSE.

When must a collector recite the "MINI MIRANDA"?

UPON INITIAL CONTACT WITH THE DEBTOR VIA WRITTEN OR VERBAL COMMUNICATION

Is it necessary to include the mini Miranda in every written communication to the debtor and / or his attorney?

YES

Explain the term "location information."

THE DEBTORS HOME PHONE NUMBER, RESIDENCE OR PLACE OF EMPLOYMENT

If an attorney represents a debtor, under what circumstances may you contact the debtor directly?

WHEN INSTRUCTED BY THE DEBTOR'S ATTORNEY OR IF THE ATTORNEY FAILS TO RESPOND TO ANY COMMUNICATION WITHIN A REASONABLE AMOUNT OF TIME.

How many times and how often can a collector contact a third party seeking location information?

ONCE, UNLESS THE INFORMATION IS OF AN INCOMPLETE NATURE

Between what hours may a collector contact a debtor?

BETWEEN 8AM AND 9PM WITHIN THE DEBTOR'S TIME ZONE

Under what circumstances must a collector cease communication with a debtor?

UPON WRITTEN NOTICE FROM THE DEBTOR OR IF THE DEBTOR HAS RETAINED THE SERVICES OF AN ATTORNEY

May a collector communicate with a debtor after receiving a cease communication request? If so, under what circumstances?

YES, ONLY ONCE TO NOTIFY THE DEBTOR OF THE COLLECTION AGENCY'S INTENTION TO EITHER CEASE COMMUNICATION OR THAT THE AGENCY IS PROCEEDING WITH THEIR EFFORTS TO COLLECT THE DEBT.

May a collector communicate with a debtor's spouse, parent or guardian (if debtor is a minor) after receiving a cease communication request from the debtor?

YES, ONLY ONCE TO NOTIFY THE DEBTOR OF THE COLLECTION AGENCY'S INTENTION TO EITHER CEASE COMMUNICATION OR THAT THE AGENCY IS PROCEEDING WITH THEIR EFFORTS TO COLLECT THE DEBT.

Under what circumstances may a collector use obscene, abusive or profane language?

ABSOLUTELY NEVER

How often may a collector make contact with a debtor?

NO MORE THAN ONCE A WEEK

Under what circumstances may a collector tell a debtor that a lawsuit will be filed to enforce collection of a debt?

ONLY WHEN THE COLLECTOR'S INTENTIONS ARE TO REFER THE ACCOUNT TO THEIR ATTORNEY FOR A SUIT

Can a collector make collect calls to a debtor? If so, under what circumstances?

NO

If a debtor disputes a debt and requests verification of the debt, when may a collector resume collection activity?

WITHIN 24 HOURS AFTER THE VALIDATION OF THE ACCOUNT HAS BEEN SENT

If a debtor has multiple debts, under what circumstances may payments be applied to a disputed account?

NONE – A PAYMENT CAN NEVER BE APPLIED TO AN ACCOUNT THAT IS IN DISPUTE

How many times may a collector contact a debtor's employer by telephone to verify employment?

ONCE, UNLESS THE INFORMATION RECEIVED IS INCOMPLETE

May a collector represent himself as an attorney if it will persuade the debtor to pay a debt?

NO

When may a collector use postcards to make demand for payment or skip tracing?

NEVER

THIS IS THE TRUE OR FALSE SECTION OF THE EXAM. PLEASE CIRCLE THE CORRECT ANSWER.

T   F   You may call a debtor every day and make demand for Payment until the debt is paid.

FALSE

T   F   You must always identify your employer when contacting a Third Party.

FALSE

T   F   You must recite the MINI MIRANDA every time you speak with The Debtor.

FALSE

T   F   If the debtor is represented by an attorney, you may contact The debtor directly if the attorney fails to respond within 3 days.

FALSE

T   F   You may call before 8am if the debtor asks you to.

TRUE

T   F   You may call the debtor at work at 12pm noon if the debtor Works at a fast food restaurant.

FALSE

T   F   After receiving a cease communication request from a debtor You may contact the debtor in writing to inform him that a lawsuit has been filed to enforce the debt.

TRUE

T   F   You can say to a debtor: "Will it be necessary for me to come To your place of employment to compel you to pay this account?"

FALSE

T   F   It is OK to talk with a debtor's priest who wants to take full responsibility for the debt of a needy person under the good Samaritan act.

FALSE

T   F   You may discuss an account with the grandson of an elderly Debtor if he tells you he is handling his grandfather's affairs.

FALSE

T   F   If the debtor is having a garage sale on Saturday and will know when it is over if she can pay you. She tells you to call her after church on Sunday. Is it OK to call her?

TRUE

T   F   If a debtor works a split shift and is always home between 6pm and 11pm you may call the debtor at 8pm.

TRUE

T	F	You can tell a debtor "you should have enough common sense to know that we mean business".

FALSE

T	F	Payments can be applied to disputed accounts to re-new the Four-year statute of limitations.

FALSE

T	F	It is OK to use several aliases so debtors won't know that you called their employer or other third parties.

FALSE

T	F	You can tell a debtor that you are referring their $99 account to The attorney's office.

YES

T	F	It is OK to ask a debtors neighbor to give your phone number to the debtor so he can return your call.

YES

T	F	If you call a debtor's work phone number and discover he works for his parents. His mother tells you she handles all of his bills. It is OK to talk to her.

FALSE

T	F	It is necessary to recite the MINI MIRANDA when speaking with the debtor's attorney.

FALSE

DO NOT SEND THIS LETTER – IT DOESN'T WORK. STATE LAWS ALLOW COLLECTION AGENCIES TO COLLECT 3ʀᴅ PARTY DEBTS – YOU CANNOT FIRE THEM.

STOP COLLECTION AGENCIES IN THEIR TRACKS!

You have the right to STOP collection agencies from ever writing or calling you again. The Fair Debt Collection Practices Act contains an empowering tool in for the consumer. By law, a collection agency must stop contacting you after they receive a letter telling them to. The body of the letter should basically read:

You are hereby notified under provision of public laws 95-109 and 99-361, also known as the Fair Debt Collection Practices act, that your services are no longer needed.

Your organization is to immediately CEASE & DESIST all attempts to

collect this debt. I will not recognize any collection agency and will

deal only with the original creditor (WHOEVER THE CREDITOR IS)

SAMPLE LETTER – DISPUTE / REQUEST FOR VALIDATION

(Collection Agency Name)   (Date)
(street Address)
(City, State, Zip Code)

Re: Dispute of Alleged Collection Account
Account: (Account Number)
Amount: (Dollar Amount)
Creditor: (Name of Original creditor)

Attention: Account Manager

It has been brought to my attention that you are attempting to collect on an account that is in legal dispute. Therefore, please consider this response as my legal dispute and request for you under public law 95-109, 15 USC 1692g. § 809 to obtain verification of this alleged debt or a copy of a judgment against me. I furthermore request the name and address of the original creditor stating that this alleged liability is mine so that civil action can be implemented to resolve this erroneous accusation, if necessary.

Any further attempt to collect and/or continue to falsely report this disputed information on my personal credit file without complying to the above stated provisions will be deemed as non-compliance and you will be held liable under 15 USC 1692 (k) (civil liability) to one or more of the following:

All actual damage sustained by a consumer as a result of such failure;

(A) Included above, additional damages allowed by the court, not exceeding $1,000; or

IF a class action is filed, such amount for each named plaintiff, recovered under subparagraph (A) of the stated Title, and an amount not to exceed the lesser of $500,000 or 1 per centum of the net worth of the debt collector; and

All cost accrued by the consumers' successful action to enforce the foregoing liability, along with attorney's fee.

It is my intention to resolve your inaccurate reporting of this activity contained on my file amiably. However, rest assured I would pursue all legal rights therein to resolve this matter.

If this liability is proven to be due, it is my intention to retire it immediately. I look forward to your response within the next 30 days. Thank you for your cooperation.

Sincerely,

(Your Name)
(Your Address)

(SAMPLE LETTER 1) – 1ˢᵀ LETTER
TO COLLECTION AGENCY

Bob Gentry
111 Value Lane
Dollar City, NV 80436

July 13, 2000

Retail Recovery Solutions
2000 18ᵗʰ St
Stockton, CA 95208

Re: Dispute of Alleged Collection Account
Account: # 4280831 - Amount: $367.17

Attention: Account Manager,

It has been brought to my attention your attempting to collect on an account that is in legal dispute. Therefore, please consider this response as my legal dispute and request for you under public law 95-109, 15 USC 1692g. § 809 to obtain verification of this alleged debt or a copy of a judgment against me. I furthermore request the name and address of the original creditor stating that this alleged liability is mine so that civil action can be implemented to resolve this erroneous accusation, if necessary.

Any further attempt to collect and/or continue to falsely report this disputed information on my personal credit file without complying to the above stated provisions will be deemed as non-compliance and you will be held liable under 15 USC 1692 (k) (civil liability) to one or more of the following:
All actual damage sustained by a consumer as a result of such failure; (A) Included above, additional damages allowed by the court, not exceeding $1,000; or
IF a class action is filed, such amount for each named plaintiff, recovered under subparagraph (A) of the stated Title, and an

amount not to exceed the lesser of $500,000 or 1 per centum of the net worth of the debt collector; and
All cost accrued by the consumers' successful action to enforce the foregoing liability, along with attorney's fee.
It is my intention to resolve your inaccurate reporting of this activity contained on my file amiably. However, rest assured I would pursue all legal rights therein to resolve this matter.

If this liability is proven to be due, it is my intention to retire it immediately. I look forward to your response within the next 30 days. Thank you for your cooperation.

Sincerely,

Bob Gentry

(SAMPLE LETTER 2)

(SAMPLE LETTER2)

Bob gentry
111 Value Lane   August 14, 2000
Dollar City, NV 80436

Retail Recovery Solutions
2000 18th St.
Stockton, CA 95208

Re: Stewart Dental Group
Account #:   056892-9
Amount Due: $73.00

To whom it may concern:

I have recently been made aware of an account that has been placed with your office for collections. Please be advised that I am unaware of ever having an account with the above-mentioned creditor and dispute it's validity. Therefore, please provide me with a copy of the itemization along with any documents I personally signed which would in any way obligate my responsibility for payment. I expect that this information will be sent to me within the next 30 days as the law requires. If you fail to send the requested information within the legal time frame, I will assume that this account will be deleted from all credit files with all credit reporting agencies and all collection efforts will cease.

I look forward to hearing from you so we may resolve this matter amicably.

Respectfully,

Bob Gentry

(SAMPLE LETTER 3)

(SAMPLE LETTER 3)

Bob gentry
111 Value Lane   September 20, 2000
Dollar City, NV 80436

Retail Recovery Solutions
2000 18th St.
Stockton, CA 95208
Attention: Collection manager

Re: Stewart Dental Group
Account #:   056892-9
Amount Due: $73.00

To whom it may concern:

This letter is to inform you that it has been over 30 days since my initial request for
documentation (see enclosure) of validation for this account. As of this date I still have
not received the information requested. Furthermore, I have been informed by the credit
reporting agencies that your company continues to confirm this account as correct and
owing. As you have not followed through with my previous request, I assume this
account will now be removed from my credit report, as the law requires. Furthermore,
please be advised that if you do not remove this account and notify me immediately in
writing of your actions, I will not only file a formal complaint with the FTC, but also
with the Office of Consumer Affairs and possibly seek legal counsel to determine what
other actions I may take.

Once again I look forward to hearing from you.

Respectfully,

Bob Gentry

(SAMPLE LETTER 4)

(SAMPLE LETTER 4)

Bob gentry
111 Value Lane   November 2, 2000
Dollar City, NV 80436

Retail Recovery Solutions
2000 18th St.
Stockton, CA 95208
Attention: Collection manager

Re: Stewart Dental Group
Account #:   056892-9
Amount Due: $73.00

To whom it may concern:

Enclosed you will find copies of previous correspondence I sent in an attempt to resolve this account within the last 90 days. Yet I still have not received the information that validates your attempt to collect this debt and your company continues to report this information to the credit reporting bureaus.
I have now retained legal counsel and am prepared to instruct my attorney to file suit against you for intentional gross negligence due to your failure to follow the laws that regulate your industry. You cannot report information to a credit-reporting agency without validating the debt within 30 days of my request. Your company is in violation of the law and of my rights as a consumer. Therefore, if I am successful at my attempts to resolve this matter legally, you may be fined of up to $1,000 for each violation and possible punitive damages for any financial duress you have caused me. Therefore, I hereby request that you do 2 things:

1. Cease all communication, written and verbal
2. Send me written correspondence and documentation that this account has been deleted from my credit report.

If I do not hear from you within 5 days from the date of this letter, I will immediately instruct my attorney to file suit against you and your company.

GOOD LUCK!

Bob Gentry

(SAMPLE LETTER 5)

Bob Gentry   July 13, 2000
111 Value Lane
Dollar City, NV 80436

Retail Recovery Solutions
2000 18ᵗʰ St
Stockton, CA 95208

Attention: Account Manager

Re: Legal Dispute of accounts: 1136817, 1133027

This letter is in response to two (2) notices that I recently received from your agency with regard to the above referenced accounts. We have a problem! You claim that you had previously notified me of these alleged liabilities and that I failed to respond. This is untrue! This is the first time that this information was brought to my attention and thereby I am legally disputing it.

Be advised that unless you provide me with evidence of your claim, the above accounts will be deemed as invalid. To my knowledge, I do not owe any outstanding liabilities, do to the fact that I was recently forced to file a Chapter 7 Bankruptcy and all of my outstanding debts were discharged through such.

I am well aware of the federal Fair Debt Collection Practices Act and request that you confirm your collection efforts before pursuing this matter any further. Be advised that I have documented your collection attempt and my dispute for future legal referencing, if necessary. As I had previously stated, I do not feel as though these are legitimate claims.

Furthermore, I will assume that this inaccurate information has not been illegally reported on my personal credit file and if so, I demand its immediate retraction. It is my intention to resolve this disputed allegation amiably however, I will pursue legal recourse if you continue to proceed with your attempts without conforming within the above stated statutes.

I will anticipate your response within thirty (30) days and will submit a copy of this dispute to the national credit reporting agencies to allow you the opportunity to retract your unjustified claim, if needed. This will also serve as legal documentation if this matter cannot be resolved between us thereby going into litigation.

I look forward to resolving this issue accordingly.

Sincerely,

Bob Gentry

(SAMPLE LETTER 6) – MEDICAL COLLECTION ACCOUNTS

Bob Gentry   July 13, 2000
111 Value Lane
Dollar City, NV 80436

Retail Recovery Solutions
2000 18th St
Stockton, CA 95208

Attention: Account Manager

Re: Legal Dispute of Accounts # 00068537588 & 00066780354

This letter is referencing several accounts in which your company is claiming as being owed by me. I had previously disputed this information with the national credit reporting agencies and requested that they investigate and confirm this disputed information or immediately delete it. I received notification from them that you confirmed the accounts as being valid.

In accordance with the federal Fair Debt Collection Practices Act, please submit to me documentation supporting your claim (notice from creditor of services rendered) and I will gladly retire this debt. I have always had medical insurance and it was my understanding that all services were covered through such. If by chance, some liabilities were not covered, upon receiving documentation supporting such, restitution will be made.

I look forward to your prompt response so that we can conclude this matter.

Sincerely,

Bob Gentry

(SAMPLE LETTER 7) – CEASE AND DESIST

Bob Gentry   July 13, 2000
111 Value Lane
Dollar City, NV 80436

Retail Recovery Solutions
2000 18th St
Stockton, CA 95208

Attention: Account Rep.

Re: Providian National Bank
Account #: 4254491400484909
Amount: $ 1,820.28

You are hereby notified under provisions of public laws 95-109 and 99-361, also known as the " Fair Debt Collection Practices Act," that your services are no longer desired.

You and your organization must "cease and desist" all attempts to collect the above debt. Failure to comply with this law will result in my immediate filing of complaints with both the Federal Trade Commission and the State Attorney General. I will pursue all criminal and civil claims against you and your organization for noncompliance of the above.

Let this correspondence also serve as warning that attempts to phone me may be recorded in order to document any illegal conversations that you may have planned in the future.

Furthermore, if any negative information is placed or appears on my credit bureau reports by your agency after receipt of this certified notice, legal suit will be filed against you and your company both personally and corporately regarding your noncompliance. I will seek any and all legal remedies, which have been made available to me by state and federal statutes.

It is my intention to resolve this claim with the original creditor and I will not tolerate your harassment any longer!

Regards,

Bob Gentry

cc: Providian National Bank; legal

(SAMPLE LETTER 8) – VERIFICATION RESPONSE

Bob Gentry   July 13, 2000
111 Value Lane
Dollar City, NV 80436

Retail Recovery Solutions
2000 18th St
Stockton, CA 95208

Re: Legal dispute of account: 9855 / Anthony, Dean M.D.
Amount: $613.16

Let this letter serve as notice that I have received your correspondence regarding my legal dispute with the national bureaus. Be advised that a copy of your correspondence has been forwarded to my legal advisor and the Federal Trade Commission. You have failed to provide me with documentation supporting your claim and have violated my rights with respect to the Fair Debt Collection Practices Act by not allowing me the required thirty (30) day time frame to dispute this alleged liability. Stating that you must re-insert this damaging and disputed reporting within five (5) days if I do not respond to your collection attempt is illegal!

I have acted within the guidelines of the federal Fair Credit Reporting Act by disputing this information with the above bureaus and the thirty (30) day time frame has well expired in which proper validation was to be produced. No other documentation has been provided to me to support this allegation other than this form letter from your company. It is my intention to retire any outstanding liability that I owe however, this does not provide me with enough validation to warrant such action.

I suggest that you provide me with the requested and required documentation so that we can conclude this matter. If this cannot be produced, this alleged liability will be deemed as unverifiable and must therefore be dismissed. If you choose to ignore both state and federal statutes by continuing to report and attempt to collect on this disputed debt, civil and corporate suit will be enforced.

Your compliance and prompt response would be appreciated.

Sincerely,

Bob Gentry
cc: FTC

(Inquiry Dispute)

(INQUIRY DISPUTE)

Bob gentry
111 Value Lane   August 14, 2000
Dollar City, NV 80436

Retail Recovery Solutions
2000 18th St.
Stockton, CA 95208

To whom it may concern:

I have recently received a copy of my credit report and have noticed an inquiry from your company on (date). Under §604(a)(2) of the fair credit-reporting act, you can only check a consumer's credit report in accordance with the written instructions of the consumer to whom it relates. I have never authorized or have given your company written or verbal permission of to inquire about my credit. Therefore, either provide me with written proof of this authorization or send me written correspondence that you have requested this inquiry deleted from my credit report.
I will withhold from invoking my legal rights for 30 days from the date of this letter. If I do not hear from you within the prescribed time frame I will assume your intentions are not to cooperate and I will take whatever action necessary to resolve this matter amicably.

Respectfully,

Bob Gentry

FILE SEGREGATION EXPOSED!

NEW ID? – BAD IDEA!

If you have filed for bankruptcy, you may be the target of a credit repair scheme called "file segregation." In this scheme you are promised a chance to hide unfavorable credit information by establishing a new credit identity. That may sound perfect, especially if you're afraid that you won't get any credit as long as bankruptcy appears on your credit record.

The problem: "file segregation" is illegal. If you use it, you could face fines or even a prison sentence.

THE PITCH: A NEW CREDIT IDENTITY

If you have filed for bankruptcy, you may receive a letter from a credit repair company that warns you about your inability to get credit cards, personal loans, or any other types of credit for 10 years. For a fee, the company promise to help you hide your bankruptcy and establish a new credit identity to use when you apply for credit. These companies also make pitches in classified ads, on radio and TV, and even over the Internet.

If you pay the fee and sign-up for the service you may be directed to apply for an Employer Identification Number (EIN) from the Internal Revenue Service. Typically, EIN's – which resemble social security numbers – are used by businesses to report financial information to the IRS and the Social Security Administration.

After you receive your EIN, the credit repair service will tell you to use it in place of your Social Security number when applying for credit.

They'll also tell you to use a new mailing address and some credit references.

THE CATCH: FALSE CLAIMS

To convince you to establish a new credit identity, the credit repair service is likely to make a variety of false claims. Listen carefully for these false claims, along with the pitch for getting a new credit identity. You'll probably hear something like this:

"You will not be able to get credit for 10 years" (the length of time the bankruptcy information may stay on your credit record).

Each creditor has its own criteria for granting credit. While one may reject your application because of bankruptcy, another may grant you credit shortly after you filed for bankruptcy. And, given a new reliable payment record, your chances of getting credit will probably increase.

"The company or file segregation program is affiliated with the federal government"

The federal government does *not* support or work with these companies that offer such programs.

"The file segregation program is legal"

It is a federal crime to make false statements on a loan or credit application. The credit repair company may advise you to do just that. It's a federal crime to misrepresent your Social Security Number. It is also a federal crime to obtain an EIN from the IRS under false pretenses. Further, You could be charged with mail or wire fraud if you use the mail or telephone to apply for credit and provide false information. Worse yet, file segregation likely would constitute civil fraud under many state laws.

RIGHTS UNDER THE CREDIT REPAIR ORGANIZATIONS ACT

This law prohibits false claims about credit repair and makes it illegal for these operations to charge you until they have preformed their services. It requires these companies to tell you about your legal rights. Credit repair companies must provide this in a written contract that also spells out just what services are to be performed, how long it will take to achieve results, the total cost and any guarantees that are offered. Under the law, these contracts also must explain that consumers have three days to cancel at no charge.

Under the law you also have the right to sue in federal court. The law allows you to seek either your actual losses or the amount you paid the company – whichever is more. You can also seek "punitive" damages: sums of money to punish the company for violating the law. The law also allows for class actions in federal court: cases where groups of consumers join together in one lawsuit. If you win, the other side has to pay your attorney's fees.

Many states have laws regulating credit repair companies, and may be helpful if you've lost money to credit repair scams.

If you've had problems with a credit repair company, report the company to your local consumer affairs office or your state attorney general. You can contact your local Attorney General Office by phone or through the National Association of Attorneys General website @ **www.naag. org**. You can also file a complaint with the Treasury Inspector General for Tax Administration by calling 1-800-336-4484.

The FTC works for the consumer to prevent fraudulent, deceptive, and unfair business practices in the marketplace and to provide information to help consumers' spot, stop, and avoid them. To file a complaint call toll-free 1-877-FTC-HELP (1-877-382-4357) or use the complaint form at www.ftc.gov.

7 WAYS TO ELIMINATE CREDIT CARD INTEREST

Many of the people I have had the pleasure of meeting feel as though their creditors have in some way taken advantage of them. However, that belief is just a misperception.

The majorities of creditors really do follow the rules and abide by the agreements they sent you when you applied for credit.

However, people are still amply upset with their creditors and want to know how they can get back at them for all the high interest rates and fees.

So here's a list of ways to help you eliminate paying interest and added fees.

PAY YOUR BILLS BEFORE THE DUE DATE

These days' credit card companies make a ton of money if you don't pay your bill on time. With late fees at or above $30 each month, it's easy to see that this is a cash cow for creditors. Creditors love people who never send their payment in until the last minute. The later you wait to send it, the greater the chance your payment will arrive past the due date. Here's what to do end your payment as soon as you can. The extra 14 cents you would have earned in interest by leaving your money in the bank isn't worth the risk of a late fee.

KEEP YOUR BALANCE BELOW THE LIMIT

If you have credit card balances that are higher than your credit limit, your creditors rush to their cash registers again. KA-CHING! While most will allow you to exceed your credit limit, they will charge you an over-limit fee each month until you bring your balance back in line. Like late fee's, over-limit charges can run as high as $30 or more and are simply putting money straight into your creditor's pockets.

PAY YOUR CREDIT CARD BILL IN FULL EACH MONTH

Using a credit card for regular purchases can be a great financial tool. You get to use someone else's money for free each month and receive a consolidated statement to help keep track of all your purchases. All you have to do is pay the bill in full before the due date. Credit cards save you from carrying a pocket full of cash and the credit card company will help you if you have a problem with a product or service you purchase with their card. You might even get rewards or perks when you use the card. By paying your account on time and in full each month you avoid paying interest, late fees and over-limit charges.

CHECK YOUR CREDIT REPORT

Your creditors have got their eyes on you and they are hoping you'll keep your eyes off your credit report. In fact, these days whole bunches of people have their eyes on your credit report. Your insurance company is watching so they can determine how much they are going to charge you for insurance. Insurance companies think that if you are having credit problems, you are an insurance risk. Okay, so maybe it's just an excuse to raise your rates. Your credit card companies also keep a close watch on your credit report. They're looking for bad marks, also. If you run into problems with one of your creditors, don't be surprised if all your credit cards get a sudden increase in interest rates. Even if you have been paying your bills on time to your other creditors, they can all raise their rates if you pay someone else late. It's not uncommon these days to see rates near or above 30 percent once your credit report starts to show late payments. If you haven't checked your credit report in a while, you don't know if it's correct or not. Just because you've been a model citizen when it comes to paying your bills doesn't mean you know if somebody else's bad habits have landed on your credit report in error. Keep in mind – statistics show that over 78% of all Americans have at least one error contained in their credit report. Here's what to do – order a copy of your credit report from Experian.com, Equifax.com and TransUnion.com. These reports will show all payment history about you. Make sure someone else's problems haven't become yours.

TAKE ADVANTAGE OF "SAME AS CASH" CREDIT TERMS

You know those furniture and electronic store ads that say you can buy the item today and not make a single payment for 90 days and they won't charge you any interest? It's true – if you play by the rules and pay off the bill before the due date, you can keep your money in the bank and use their money for free. The creditors are hoping that most people won't pay it off before the due date. Then, not only will they get to charge interest in the future, but they'll also whip out their calculators and figure out how much interest has racked up during the "free 90 days". If you don't pay your balance off before that 90-day mark, all of that newly accrued interest will land on your bill. Here's what to do – pay off any extended credit agreements within the "same as cash" period.

CONSOLIDATE YOUR DEBT

If you don't want your high interest rate creditors to get their hands on your money, pay it off with low interest rate debt. If you have equity in your home, you can potentially tap into that cash with a low fixed interest rate loan and pay off your bills. Of course this trick only works if you don't run up your balances again.

USE CASH ADVANCES WISELY

If you need cash, think twice before taking a cash advance from your credit card. Cash advances are treated differently from regular purchases. Typically creditors charge higher interest rates for cash advances and the interest begins accruing right away. Some creditors even add a cash advance fee. Be sure you understand your cardholder agreement because your regular monthly payment might be applied only to your revolving balance. Unless you understand exactly how your future monthly payments will be applied to the outstanding balance, you will be shocked that your cash advance won't be paid off for years.

You see if you owe $1,000 as a revolving balance and took out a $500 cash advance you would have to send the entire $1,500 to pay off the cash advance. The cash advance portion of your bill is usually the last place your payment is applied. Let's say the following month you sent $500 to pay off the cash advance, the payment will most likely be applied to $500 of the revolving balance due and the cash advance amount will continue to build interest at the higher rate. However, your creditor might have a special policy to allow you to pay off the cash advance portion of the bill first but you have got to do your homework to find out exactly how. Sometimes you can do it by making the regular monthly revolving payment and send the cash advance pay off separately with a special mailing address. Always read your credit card owners manual before accepting any offer.

SECURED CREDIT CARD MARKETING SCAMS

Ads like this may appeal to you if you have a poor credit history or no credit at all. Beware! While secured credit cards can be an effective way to build or re-establish your credit history, some marketers of secured credit cards make deceptive advertising claims to entice you to respond to their ads.

SECURED VS. UNSECURED CARDS

Secured and unsecured cards can be used to pay for goods and services. However, a secured credit card requires you to open and maintain a savings account as security for your line of credit; an unsecured credit card does not.

The required savings deposit for a secured card may range from a few hundred to several thousands of dollars. Your credit line is a percentage of your deposit, typically 50 to 100 percent. Usually, a bank will pay interest on your deposit. In addition, you also may have to pay application and processing fees – sometimes totaling hundreds of dollars. Before you apply, be sure to ask what the total fees are and whether they will be refunded if you're denied a card. Typically, a secured card requires an annual fee and has a higher interest rate than an unsecured card.

DECEPTIVE ADS AND SCAMS

The Federal Trade Commission (FTC) has taken action against companies that deceptively advertise major credit cards through television, newspapers and postcards. The ads may offer unsecured cards, secured cards or not specify a card type. The ads usually lead you to believe you can get a card simply by calling the number listed. Sometimes the number is not toll-free but a 900 number service for which you are charged for just making the call. Then, once the call is made, it could be an automated recording instructing you to leave your name and address to receive a credit application or just give you a list of banks offering secured credit cards. It also may tell you to call another 900 number – at an additional charge – for more information.

- Deceptive ads often leave out important information such as:
- The cost of the 900 call – which can range in excess of $2 or more;
- The required security deposit, application and processing fee;
- Eligibility requirements like income or age;
- An annual fee or the fact that the secured card has a higher than average interest rate on any balance.

HOW TO AVOID THE SCAM

To avoid being victimized, look for the following signs:
1. Offers of easy credit. No one can guarantee to get you credit. Before deciding whether to give you a credit card, legitimate credit providers examine your credit report.
2. A call to a 900 number for a credit card. You pay for calls with a 900 prefix – and you may never receive a credit card.
3. Credit cards offered by "credit repair" companies or "credit clinics." These businesses also may offer to clean up your credit history for a fee. However, you can correct genuine mistakes or outdated information yourself by contacting credit bureaus directly. Remember that only time and good credit habits will restore your credit worthiness.

CREDIT REPORTING

If you're considering a secured card as a way to build or re-establish a credit record, make sure the issuer reports to a credit bureau. Companies called credit bureaus maintain your credit history; they collect information reported to them by banks, mortgage companies, department stores, and other creditors. If your card issuer doesn't report to a bureau, the card won't help you build credit history.

FOR MORE INFORMATION

To build a credit record, you may want to apply for a charge card or a small loan at a local store or lending institution. Ask if the creditor reports transactions to a credit bureau. If they do – and if you pay back your debts regularly – you will build good credit history.

If your having problems paying your bills, you may want to contact a non-profit credit counseling service. Non-profit organizations in every state counsel consumers who are in debt. Counselors try to arrange a repayment plan that is acceptable to you and your creditors. They can also help set-up a realistic budget. These counseling services are offered at little or no cost to consumers. You can find the nearest service to you by checking the White Pages of your telephone directory.
Sometimes, universities, military bases, credit unions and housing authorities, operate non-profit counseling programs. Or you can check with your local bank or consumer protection office to see if it has a list of reputable low-cost financial counseling services.

WHERE TO COMPLAIN

If you have problems or questions about a secured credit card marketer, contact your local consumer protection agency or state Attorney General's office. You may also file a complaint with the FTC. The FTC works for the consumer to prevent fraudulent, deceptive and unfair business practices in the marketplace and to provide information to help consumers spot, stop and avoid them. To file a complaint or to get free information you can call toll-free @ 1-877-FTC-HELP (1-877-382-4357), or use the complaint form at www.ftc.gov.

BEST OVERALL CARD

For those people who carry balances KCCC has calculated an annual cost to maintain a standard credit card with an introductory rate. The analysis was based on the following spending habits and assumptions: 1) Average balance of $2,000 is held on account for a 12-month period. 2) The annual fee, if applicable, is applied in month one. 3) All payments are made on time and no late fees are assessed. Most of the cards surveyed are nationally available. There are a few exceptions that are noted. Before signing an application, verify all information -- it can suddenly change. *Survey date is November 1999.

Best overall credit card with an introductory rate

Issuer/ Phone/ Card Type (MasterCard/ Visa)	Intro Rate/ Intro Period (mos)	Use of Funds	Rate After Intro	Fixed or Var	Index (Variable) Margin Annual Fee	Interest Free Days/ From	Area Available	Cost Over Next 12 Month
Bank One Chicago, IL 888-221-9067 Cards: MC/V	3.90% 6	Purchase - Balance Transfer	9.99%	F	NA/ NA/ $0	20 billing	National	$ 138.90
Chase Manhattan Bank USA Wilmington, DE 800-441-7681 Cards: MC/V	3.99% 9	Purchase - Balance Transfer	17.74%	V	Prime rate/ 9.49%/ $0	22 billing	National	$ 148.55
Security First Network Bank Atlanta, GA 800-736-2321 Cards: V	3.90% 6	Purchase - Cash - Balance Transfer	12.90%	F	NA/ NA/ $0	25 billing	Regional	$ 168.00
Main Street Bank Covington, GA 888-712-7915 Cards: MC	4.90% 6	Purchase - Balance Transfer	12.90%	F	NA/ NA/ $0	25 billing	National	$ 178.00

Astoria Federal Savings Wilmington, DE 800-955-9900 Cards: V	2.90%5	Purchase - Balance Transfer	13.24%V	Prime rate/ 4.99%/ $0	20 billing	Regional	$ 178.63
National City Bank Cleveland, OH 800-282-7541 Cards: V	3.90%6	Purchase - Balance Transfer	15.74%V	Prime rate/ 7.49%/ $0	25 billing	Regional	$ 196.40
AFBA Industrial Bank Colorado Springs, CO² 800-776-2265 Cards: MC/V	8.50%6	Purchase - Cash - Balance Transfer	11.40%V	Prime rate/ 2.90%/ $0	25 billing	National	$ 199.00
SunTrust Bank Orlando, FL 800-786-8787 Cards: MC/V	4.90%6	Purchase - Cash - Balance Transfer	15.24%V	Prime rate/ 6.99%/ $0	25 billing	National	$ 201.40
Am Trust Bank Boca Raton, FL 888-268-7878 Cards: MC/V	6.90%6	Purchase - Balance Transfer	12.00%V	Prime rate/ 3.75%/ $18	25 billing	Not Available: MD NM NY NV UT	$ 207.00
Ohio Savings Bank Cleveland, OH 800-987-6446 Cards: MC/V	6.90%6	Purchase - Balance Transfer	12.00%V	Prime rate/ 3.75%/ $18	25 billing	Not Available: MD NM NY NV UT	$ 207.00

Grace period (interest free days) applies to purchases only; cash advances frequently are charged interest from the date of transaction.

Additional fees may be charged such as for exceeding a credit line, making a payment late, obtaining a cash advance, making an ATM transaction, or if a check is returned
[1] **Introductory rate may range** [2] **Rate after introductory will not adjust lower (Floor)**

FICO SCORES

Understanding the crossroads that lead to explaining the score

WHAT MAKES UP A FICO SCORE?

→ 35% = based on payment history (i.e. on-time pays or delinquencies).

→ 30% = capacity (capacity is King).

→ 15% = length of established credit history.

→ 10% = accumulation of debt in the last 12 – 18 months. (# of inquires, opening dates).

→ 10% = mix of credit – installment (raises) vs. revolving (lowers) - # of finance company loans, the more you have, the lower the score.

WHAT ACTIONS WILL HURT THE SCORE?

→ Missing payments, regardless of the amount – It will take 24 months to restore credit with one late pay.

→ Credit cards at capacity – Maxed out credit cards.

→ Closing credit cards out – This lowers available capacity.

→ Shopping for credit excessively

→ Opening numerous trades in a short period of time.

→ Having more revolving loans in relation to installment loans.

→ Borrowing from finance companies.

WHAT DOESN'T AFFECT THE SCORE?

→ Debt ratio

→ Income

→ Length of residence

→ Length of employment

APPROXIMATE CREDIT WEIGHT FOR EACH YEAR:

→ 40% = current to 12 months.

→ 30% = 13 – 24 months.

→ 20% = 25 – 36 months.

→ 10% = 37 + months.

HOW TO IMPROVE THE SCORE:

→ Pay down credit cards.

→ Do not close credit card accounts (decreases capacity).

→ Make all payments on-time.

→ Slow down on opening accounts.

→ Move revolving debt to installment debt.

→ Acquire a solid credit history with years of experience.

PAYDAY LOANS = COSTLY CASH

"I just need enough cash to hold me over until payday."

"GET CASH UNTIL PAYDAY! $100 OR MORE... FAST."

The ads are on radio, television, the Internet and even in the mail. They refer to payday loans that come at a very high price.

Check cashers, finance companies and others are making small, short-term, high interest rate loans that go by a variety of names: Payday loans, cash advance loans, check advance loans, post-dated check loans or deferred deposit loans.

Usually, a borrower writes a personal check payable to the lender for the amount he or she wishes to borrow plus a fee. The company gives the borrower the amount of the check minus the fee. Fees charged for payday loans are usually a percentage of the face value of the check or a fee charged per amount borrowed – say, for every $50 or $100 loaned. And, if you extend or "roll-over" the loan – say for an extra two weeks – you will pay the fees for each extension. Under the Truth in Lending Act, the cost of payday loans like other types of credit must be disclosed. Among other information, you must receive in writing the finance charge (a dollar amount) and the annual percentage rate or APR (the cost of credit on a yearly basis).

A cash advance loan secured by a personal check – such as a payday loan – is very expensive credit. Let's say you write a personal check for $115 to borrow $100 for up to 14 days. The check casher or payday lender agrees to hold the check until your next payday. At the time, depending on the particular plan, the lender deposits the check; you redeem the check by paying the $115 in cash, or you rollover the check by paying a fee to extend the loan for another two weeks. In this example, the cost of the initial loan is a $15 finance charge and 391% APR. If you rollover the loan three times, the finance charge would climb to $60 just to borrow $100.

ALTERNATIVE TO PAYDAY LOANS

There are options. Consider the possibilities before choosing a payday loan:

- When you need credit, shop carefully. Compare offers and look for the credit offers with the lowest APR – consider a small loan from your credit union or a small loan company, an advance from your employer or a loan from family or friends. A cash advance on a credit card also may be a possibility, but it may have a higher interest rate than other sources of funds, find out the terms before you decide. Also, a local community-based organization may make small business loans to individuals.

- Compare the APR and the finance charge (which includes loan fees, interest and other types of credit costs) of credit offers to get the lowest cost.

- Ask your creditors for more time to pay your bills. Find out what they will charge for that service – as a late charge, an additional finance charge or a higher interest rate.

- Make a realistic budget and figure your monthly and daily expenditures. Avoid unnecessary purchases – even small daily items – their costs add up. Also, build some savings to help avoid borrowing emergencies and unexpected expenses and other items. For example – by putting the amount of the fee that would be paid on a typical $300 payday loan in a savings account for six months, you would have extra dollars available. This can give you a buffer against financial emergencies.

- Find out if you have or can get overdraft protection on your checking account. If you are regularly using most or all of the funds in your account, and if you make a mistake in your checking account ledger or records, overdraft protection can help you from further credit problems.

- If you need help working out a debt repayment plan with creditors or developing a budget, contact your local consumer credit counseling service. There are non-profit groups in every state that offer credit guidance to consumers. These services are available at little or no cost to you.

- If you decide you must use a payday loan company, borrow only as much as you can afford to pay with your next paycheck and still have enough to make it to the next payday.

TO COMPLAIN/FOR MORE INFORMATION

If you believe a lender has violated the Truth in Lending Act, you can file a complaint with the FTC. The FTC works for the consumer to prevent fraudulent, deceptive and unfair business practices in the marketplace and to provide information to help consumers spot, stop and avoid them. To file a complaint or to get free information on consumer issues, visit www.ftc.gov or call toll-free at 1-877-FTC-HELP (1-877-382-4257).

VEHICLE REPOSSESSION

When you finance or lease a car, truck or other vehicle your creditor or lesser holds important rights on the vehicle until you've made the last loan payment or fully paid off your leasing obligation. These rights are established by the signed contract and by state law. For example, if your payments are late or you default on your contract in any way, your creditor or lesser may have the right to repossess your car. In many states, creditors or lesser can do this legally without going to court or warning you in advance, as long as they do not breach the peace. In addition, your creditor or lesser may be able to sell your contract to a third party, called an assignee, who may have the same rights and responsibilities as the original creditor or lesser.

However, some state laws limit the ways a creditor or lesser can repossess and sell a vehicle to reduce or eliminate your debt. If any rules are violated, the creditor or lesser may be required to pay you damages.

SEIZING THE VEHICLE

In many states, your creditor or lesser has legal authority to seize your vehicle as soon as you default on your loan or lease. Because state laws differ, read your contract to find out what constitutes a default. In some states, failures to make a payment on time or meet your contractual responsibilities are considered defaults.

If your creditor or lesser has agreed to change your payment date or any other contractual obligations, it's possible that the terms of your original contract may no longer apply. Such a change may be made orally or in writing. It's best to get any changes in writing because oral agreements are difficult to prove.

If you default on your loan, the law in most states allows the creditor or lesser to repossess your vehicle. In some states, creditors or lesser are allowed on your property to seize the vehicle without letting you know in advance.

At the same time, the law usually doesn't allow your creditor or lesser to commit a breach of the peace in connection with repossession. In some states, removing the vehicle from a closed garage without your permission may constitute a breach of peace.

Creditors or lesser who breach the peace in seizing the vehicle may be required to compensate you if they harm your property.

SELLING THE CAR

Once the vehicle has been repossessed, your creditor or lesser may decide to keep the vehicle as compensation of your debt or sell the vehicle in either a public or private sale. In some states, your creditor or lesser must let you know what will happen to the vehicle. For example, if a creditor or lesser chooses to sell the vehicle at public auction, state law may require that the creditor or lesser tell you the date of the sale so that you can attend and participate in the bidding. If the vehicle is to be sold privately, you may have a right to know the date it will be sold.

In either of these circumstances, you may be entitled to buy back the vehicle by paying the full amount you owe, plus any expenses connected with its repossession, such as storage and preparation for sale. In some states, the law allows you to reinstate your contract – reclaim the vehicle by paying the amount you owe, as well as any repossession related expenses (such as attorney fees). If you reclaim the vehicle, you must make your payments on time and meet the terms of your reinstated or renegotiated contract to avoid another repossession.

The sale of a repossessed vehicle must be conducted in a commercially reasonable manner – according to standard custom in a particular business or an established market. For example, the sale price might not be the highest possible price – or even what you may consider a good price – but a sale price far below fair market value may indicate that the sale was not commercially reasonable. Depending on state law, failure to sell the vehicle in a commercially reasonable manner may give you either a claim against your creditor or lesser for damages or a defense against deficiency judgment – a court order mandating you to pay the debt you owe.

Regardless of the method used to dispose of a repossessed vehicle, a creditor or lesser usually may not keep or sell any personal property found inside. Since state laws vary, check to see if this applies in your state. State laws also may require your creditor or lesser to use reasonable care to prevent others from removing your property from the repossessed vehicle. If you find that your creditor or lesser cannot account for articles left in the vehicle, talk to an attorney about whether your state offers a right to compensate.

PAYING THE DEFICIENCY

A deficiency is an amount you still owe on your contract after your creditor or lesser sells the vehicle and applies the amount received to your unpaid obligation. For example, if you owe $2,500 on the vehicle and your creditor or lesser sells the vehicle for $1,500, the deficiency balance is $1,000 plus any other fees you owe under the contract, such as those related to the repossession and early termination of your lease or early payoff of your financing. In most states, a creditor or lesser who has followed the proper procedures for repossession and sale is allowed to sue you for a deficiency judgment to collect the remaining amount you owed on your credit or lease contract.

Depending on your states law and other factors, if you are sued for a deficiency judgment, you should be notified of the date of the court hearing. This may be your only opportunity to present any legal defense. If your creditor or lesser breached the peace when seizing the vehicle or failed to sell the vehicle in a commercially reasonable manner, you may have a legal defense against deficiency judgment. An attorney will be able to tell you whether you have grounds to contest a deficiency judgment.

Talking with your Creditor or Lesser

It's easier to try to prevent vehicle repossession from taking place than it is to dispute it afterward. Contact your creditor or lesser when you realize you will be late with a payment. Many creditors or lesser will work with you if they believe you will be able to pay soon, even if slightly late.

Sometimes you may be able to negotiate a delay in your payment or revised schedule of payments. If you reach an agreement to modify your original contract, get it in writing to avoid questions later.

Still your creditor or lesser may refuse to accept late payments or make other changes in your contract and may demand that you return the vehicle. By voluntarily agreeing to repossession, you may reduce your creditor or lessor's expenses, which you would be responsible for paying. Remember that even if you return the vehicle voluntarily, you are still responsible for paying any deficiency on your credit or lease contract, and your creditor or lesser still may enter the late payments and/or repossession on your credit report.

If you need help in dealing with your credit or lease contract, consider using a credit counseling service. There are non-profit organizations in every state that advise consumers on debt management. Counselors often try to arrange a repayment plan that is acceptable to you and your creditors. They also can help you set up a realistic budget and plan expenditures. These counseling services are offered at little or no cost to consumers. Check your telephone directory for the office nearest you.

In addition, universities, military bases, credit unions and housing authorities operate nonprofit counseling programs. They also are likely to charge little or nothing for their assistance. Or check with your local bank or consumer protection office to see if it has a list of reputable, low-cost financial counseling service.

TO COMPLAIN OR FOR MORE INFORMATION

If you believe a lender has violated the Truth in Lending Act, you can file a complaint with the FTC. The FTC works for the consumer to prevent fraudulent, deceptive and unfair business practices in the marketplace and to provide information to help consumers spot, stop and avoid them. To file a complaint or to get free information on consumer issues, visit **www.ftc.gov** or call toll-free at 1-877-FTC-HELP (1-877-382-4257).

ID THEFT
WHAT'S IT ALL ABOUT?

The 1990's spawned a new variety of crooks called identity thieves. What's their stock in trade? Your everyday transactions, which usually reveal bits of your personal information such as your bank and credit card account numbers, your income, your social security number (SSN) or your name, address and phone numbers. An identity thief obtains some piece of your sensitive information and uses it without your knowledge to commit fraud or theft.

Identity theft is a serious crime. People whose identities have been stolen can spend months or even years, and their hard earned money cleaning up the mess the thieves have made of their good name and credit record. Some victims have lost job opportunities, been refused loans for education, housing or cars, or even been arrested for crimes they didn't commit.

Can you prevent identity theft from occurring? As with any crime, you cannot completely control whether you will become a victim. But, according to the Federal Trade Commission (FTC), you can minimize your risk by managing your personal information cautiously and with heightened sensitivity.

HOW IDENTITY THEFT OCCURS

Skilled identity thieves use a variety of methods to gain access to your personal information. For example:

- They get information from businesses or other institutions by:
    - Stealing records from their employer
    - Bribing an employee who has access to these records
    - Hacking into the organizations computers

- They rummage through your trash, or the trash of businesses or dumps in a practice known as "dumpster diving."

- They obtain credit reports by abusing their employer's authorized access to credit reports or by posing as a landlord, employer, or someone else who may have a legal right to the information.

- They steal credit and debit card numbers as your card is processed by using a special information storage device in a practice known as "skimming."

- They steal wallets and purses containing identification and credit and bank cards.

- They steal mail, including bank and credit card statements, pre-approved credit offers, new checks, or tax information.

- They complete a change of address form to divert your mail to another location.

- They steal personal information from your home.

- They scam information from you by posing as a legitimate business person or government official.

Once identity thieves have your personal information, they may:

- Go on a spending spree using your credit and debit account numbers to buy "big-ticket" items like computers that they can easily sell.

- Open a new credit card account, using your name, date of birth, and SSN. When they don't pay the bills, the delinquent account is reported on your credit report.

- Change the mailing address on your credit card account. The imposter then runs up charges on the account. Because the bills are being sent to the new address, it may take some time before you realize there's a problem.

- Take out auto loans in your name.

- Establish phone or wireless service in your name.

- Counterfeit checks or debit cards, and drain your bank account.

- Open a bank account in your name and write bad checks on that account.

- File for bankruptcy under your name to avoid paying debts they've incurred, or to avoid eviction.

- Give your name to the police during an arrest. If they are released and don't show up for their court date, an arrest warrant can be issued in your name.

HOW CAN I TELL IF I'M A VICTIM OF IDENTITY THEFT?

Monitor the balances of your financial accounts. Look for unexplained charges or withdrawals. Other indications of identity theft can be:

- Failing to receive bills or other mail signaling an address change by the identity thief.

- Receiving credit cards for which you did not apply.

- Denial of credit for no apparent reason.

- Receiving calls from debt collectors or companies about merchandise or services you didn't buy.

ARE THERE ANY OTHER STEPS I CAN TAKE?

If an identity thief is opening new credit accounts in your name, these accounts are likely to show up on your credit report. You can find out by ordering a copy of your credit report from any of three major credit bureaus. If you find inaccurate information, check your reports from the other two credit bureaus. Of course, some inaccuracies on your credit reports may be because of computer, clerical, or other errors and may not be a result of identity theft. If your personal information has been stolen, you may want to check all of your reports more frequently for the first year. Federal law allows credit bureaus to charge a fee for a copy of your credit report, or you can get one free of charge once a year by going to www.annualcreditreport.com. If you don't have Internet access you can order your report from:

Equifax – www.equifax.com
1-800-685-1111

Experian – www.experian.com
1-888-397-3742

Trans Union – www.transunion.com
1-800-916-8800

MANAGING YOUR PERSONAL INFORMATION

So, how can a responsible consumer minimize the risk of identity theft, as well as the potential for damage? When it involves your personal information, exercise caution and good sense.

What to do RIGHT NOW...

Place passwords on your credit card, bank and phone accounts. Avoid using easily available information like your mother's maiden name, your birth date, the last four digits of your SSN or your phone number, or a series of consecutive numbers. When you're asked for your mother's maiden name on an application for a new account, try using a password instead.

Secure personal information in your home, especially if you have roommates, employ outside help, or having service work done in your home.

Ask about information security procedures in your workplace. Find out who has access to your personal information and verify that your records are kept in a secure location. Ask about the disposal procedures for those records as well.

Everyday Diligence...

Don't give out personal information on the phone, through the mail or over the Internet unless you've initiated the contact or are sure you know who you are dealing with. Identity thieves can be skilled liars, and may pose as representatives of banks, Internet Service Providers (ISP's) or even government agencies to get you to reveal identifying information. Before you divulge any personal information, confirm that you are dealing with a legitimate representative of a legitimate organization. Double check by calling customer service using the number on your account statement or the telephone book.

Guard your mail and trash from theft. Deposit outgoing mail in post office collection boxes or at your local post office instead of an unsecured mailbox. Remove mail from your mailbox promptly. If you're planning to be away from home and pick-up your mail, call the U.S. Postal Service at 1-800-275-8777 to ask for a vacation hold. To thwart a thief who may pick through your trash or recycling bins, tear or shred your charge receipts, copies of credit applications or offers, insurance forms, physicians statements, checks and bank statements, and expired charge cards.

Before revealing any identifying information (for example, on an application) asks how it will be used and secured, and whether it will be shared with others. Find out if you have a say about the use of your information. For example, can you choose to have it kept confidential?

Keep your SSN card in a secure place and give your SSN only when absolutely necessary. Ask to use other types of identifiers when possible. If your state uses your SSN as your driver's license number, ask to substitute another number.

Limit the identification information and the number of credit and debit cards that you carry to what you'll actually need and keep your purse or wallet in a safe place at work.

Consider Your Computer...
Your computer can be a goldmine of personal information to an identity thief. Here's how you can safeguard your computer and the personal information it stores:

- Update your virus protection software regularly. Computer viruses can have damaging effects, including introducing program code that causes your computer to send out files or other stored information. Look for security repairs and patches you can download from your operating system's website.

- Don't download files from strangers or click on hyperlinks from people you don't know. Opening a file could expose your system to a computer virus or a program that could hijack your modem.

- Use a firewall, especially if you have a high-speed or "always on" connection to the Internet. The firewall allows you to limit uninvited access to your computer. Without a firewall, hackers can take over your computer and access sensitive information.

- Use a secure browser – software that encrypts or scrambles information you send over the Internet – to guard the safety of your online transactions. When you're submitting information, look for the "lock" icon on the status bar. It's a symbol that your information is secure during transmission.

- Try not to store financial information on your laptop unless absolutely necessary. If you do, use a "strong" password – that is, a combination of letters (upper and lower case), numbers and symbols.

- Avoid using an automatic log-in feature that saves your user name and password; and always log-off when you're finished. If your laptop gets stolen, the thief will have a hard time accessing sensitive information.

- Delete any personal information stored on your computer before you dispose of it. Use a "wipe" utility program, which overwrites the entire hard drive and makes the files unrecoverable.

- Read website privacy policies. They should answer questions about access to and accuracy, security, and control of personal information the site collects, as well as how sensitive information will be used, and whether it will be provided to third parties.

IF YOUR IDENTITY'S BEEN STOLEN

Even if you've been very careful about keeping your personal information to yourself, an identity thief can strike. If you suspect that your personal information has been used to commit fraud or theft, take the following steps right away. Remember to follow-up all calls in writing; send your letter by certified mail, return receipt requested, so you can document what the company received and when; and keep copies for your files.

1. Place a fraud alerts on your credit reports and review your credit reports.

   Call the toll-free fraud number of any one of the 3 major credit bureaus to place a fraud alert on your credit report. This can help prevent an identity thief from opening additional accounts in your name. As soon as the credit bureau confirms your fraud alert, the other 2 credit bureaus will automatically be notified to place fraud alerts on your credit report, and all three reports will be sent to you free of charge.

2. Close any accounts that have been tampered with or opened fraudulently.

   Credit Accounts – credit accounts include all accounts with banks, credit card companies and other lenders, and phone companies, utilities, ISP's, and other service providers.

   If your closing existing accounts and opening new ones, use new personal identification numbers (PIN's) and passwords.

   If there are fraudulent charges or debits, ask the company about the following forms for disputing those transactions:

   For new unauthorized accounts, ask if the company accepts ID Theft Affidavit (available at **www.ftc.gov/bcp/conline/pubs/ credit/affidavit.pdf**). If they don't ask the representative to send you the company's fraud dispute forms. For your existing accounts, ask the representative to send you the company's fraud dispute forms. If your ATM card has been lost, stolen or otherwise compromised, cancel the card as soon as you can. Get a new card with a new PIN.

   Checks – If your checks have been stolen or misused, close the account and ask your bank to notify the appropriate check verification service. While no federal law limits your losses if someone steals your checks and forges your signature, state laws may protect you. Most states hold the bank responsible for losses from a forged check, but they also require you to take reasonable care of your account. For example, you may be held responsible for the forgery if you fail to notify the bank in a timely manner that a check was lost or stolen. Contact your state banking or consumer protection agency for more information.

You also should contact these major check verification companies. Ask that retailers who use their databases not accept your checks.

TeleCheck   1-800-710-9898
Certegy, Inc   1-800-437-5120
Call SCAN   1-800-262-7771 to find out if the identity thief has been passing bad checks in your name.

3. File a report with your local police or the police in the community where the identity theft took place.

    Keep a copy of the report. You may need it to validate your claims to creditors. If you can't get a copy, at least get the report number.

4. File a complaint with the FTC.

    By sharing your identity theft complaint with the FTC, you will provide important information that can help law enforcement officials track down identity thieves and stop them. The FTC also can refer victim complaints to other appropriate government agencies and companies for further action. The FTC enters the information you provide into our secure database.

A SPECIAL WORD ABOUT SOCIAL SECURITY NUMBERS

Very likely, your employer and financial institution will need your SSN for wage and tax reporting purposes. Other private businesses may ask you for your SSN to do a credit check, such as when you apply for a car loan. Sometimes, however, they simply want your SSN for general record keeping. If someone asks for your SSN, ask the following questions:

- Why do you need it?
- How will it be used?
- How do you protect it from being stolen?
- What will happen if I don't give it to you?

If you don't provide your SSN, some businesses may not provide you with the service or benefit you want. Getting satisfactory answers to your questions will help you to decide whether you want to share your SSN with the business.

To file a complaint or to learn more about the FTC's Privacy Policy, visit **www.consumer.gov/idtheft**. If you don't have access to the Internet, you can call the FTC's Identity Theft Hotline toll-free at 1-877-IDTHEFT.

ABOUT THE AUTHOR

In the beginning, at the ripe-old-age of 22 I was newly married and a soon to be father of one. I never thought about the financial responsibilities of being a husband let alone a father and I had no idea the ramifications of what it would be like if I could never pay my bills, nor did I care, everything seemed to be okay. I had a perfect credit rating and had never had to deal with collection agencies before. I was working 14 hours a day, six days a week as a manager for a popular restaurant chain in Seattle Washington and I was doing fine financially, although I could barely keep my head above water, I was still making enough money each month to get by. However, I didn't have a very good health insurance plan and 3 months later when my daughter was born, well that was it. I couldn't make enough money to pay all the bills and still be able to do the things I wanted. As a matter of fact I found myself struggling from one day to the next. Now at the time I had no idea what my rights were when it came to dealing with collection agencies and believe me when I tell you, there were collections agencies calling… so it came, call after call, letter after letter, demand after demand seemed everyone wanted my money, and there was just not enough to go around. I mean I had a family and I still had to put food on the table and diapers on the baby. Things got so bad my wife and I stopped answering the phone and we prayed for everyday to be Sunday so there was no mail or calls as most collection agencies and creditors are closed on Sunday. My credit had finally nosed dived into oblivion. The end was near and bankruptcy seemed inevitable.

Then one day I received a letter from a collection agency offering me a settlement. I was so thrilled and relieved at the prospect of maybe being able to pay one of what seemed like a hundred different medical bills, I anxiously called them. I discussed my account with the collector and all the options available to me. After making the arrangements for payment, I started asking questions to the collector as to what it was like working for a collection agency. I was amazed and a little skeptical as the collector told me about how she only works 40 hours a week and was making more money in a month than I make in 3 months, combined. Seems I was in the wrong line of work. So, I decided to see if maybe I could break into the collection business. I sent resumes out to all the collection agencies in the area where I lived and was lucky to receive a job working for one of the largest agencies in the state.

A career is born. I started working in the collection industry in June of 1986 and I will never forget what that collector told me on that faithful day. She told me that if you ever want to make a lot of money and work fewer hours, become a bill collector. Now, before trashing the collection industry, it is important to understand that the debt collection industry is very much needed in this day and age. Without them, we would all be paying higher prices for everything as businesses try to recoup their losses from the consumers who didn't pay. So, I became a bill collector and she was right, I made a lot of money in this business. However, the two things she didn't tell me are the 2 reasons I'm not in that industry today. First, she neglected to tell me how depressing this business is, and the level of stress you go through is enormous. You see, as a bill collector you work on commissions, that means you earn a percentage of whatever amount of money you collect from one month to the next. So, if you have a bad month, you don't get paid, that's pretty stressful. Plus, the day-to-day fact that you're dealing with people whom for the most part cannot genuinely pay their bills is very depressing. I mean most consumers don't wake up in the morning and say "hey-let's see if I can create a bill I can't afford to pay". Therefore, once again, I have decided to change careers. I now own my own consulting firm helping people like you, understand your rights when collection agencies come knocking. However, I do have over 18 years of experience within every aspect of the collection industry, from the guy making the collection phone calls to the guy running the entire operation to the computer equipment they use. I know everything there is to know about this industry, and it's time I shared my secrets with you!

www.ingramcontent.com/pod-product-compliance
Lightning Source LLC
Chambersburg PA
CBHW022000170526
45157CB00003B/1084